GLOBETROTTER™

Travel Guide

BARCELONA

SUE BRYANT

NEW
HOLLAND

NEW
HOLLAND

★★★ Highly recommended
★★ Recommended
★ See if you can

This edition first published in 2001
by New Holland Publishers (UK) Ltd
London • Cape Town • Sydney • Auckland
First published in 1997
10 9 8 7 6 5 4 3 2

Garfield House, 86 Edgware Road
London W2 2EA
United Kingdom

80 McKenzie Street
Cape Town 8001
South Africa

14 Aquatic Drive
Frenchs Forest, NSW 2086
Australia

218 Lake Road
Northcote, Auckland
New Zealand

ISBN 1 85974 850 3

Commissioning Editor: Tim Jollands
Manager Globetrotter Maps: John Loubser
Managing Editor: Thea Grobbelaar
Editors: Tarryn Berry, Susannah Coucher, Peter Duncan
Editorial Assistant: Rowena Curtis

Design and DTP: Sonya Cupido, Éloïse Moss
Cartographers: Elaine Fick, Éloïse Moss

Reproduction by Hirt & Carter (Pty) Ltd, Cape Town
Printed and bound by Times Offset (M) Sdn. Bhd.,
Malaysia.

Although every effort has been made to ensure
accuracy of facts, telephone and fax numbers in this
book, the publishers will not be held responsible for
changes that occur at the time of going to press.

Acknowledgements:
The author wishes to thank the Hotel Rey Juan
Carlos I; the Hotel Arts; and for assistance with
research, Gretchen Thornburn. The publishers
thank Transports Municipals de Barcelona SA for
their help in the preparation of this book.

Photographic Credits:
Sue Bryant, pages 56, 66, 70, 71 (bottom), 72, 86, 87;
Compliments of Andorra Delegation in Great Britain,
page 113; Compliments of Port Aventura, page 102;
Peter Duncan, title page, pages 4, 6, 12, 13, 18, 23
(bottom), 28, 55, 57, 73, 74, 83, 88, 91; LF/Xavier
Catalan, pages 9, 15, 19, 24, 25, 26, 27, 29, 39, 40, 45,
49, 50, 58, 77, 82, 90, 92, 94, 97, 100, 101, 107, 109;
LF/Sue Davies, pages 62, 65; LF/Sally-Anne Fison,
pages 53, 79; LF/S.Kay, page 104; LF/Emma Lee,
pages 8, 108; LF/Sheila Terry, pages 110, 111; LF/Flora
Torrance, page 81; RHPL, pages 16, 37, 71 (top), 105;
RHPL/Nigel Blythe, page 36; RHPL/ Robert Frerck,
page 23 (top), 34, 42, 78, 93, 99; RHPL/Gavin Hellier,
page 32; RHPL/Michael Jenner, pages 17, 60;
RHPL/Rolf Richardson, page 68; RHPL/Peter
Scholey, page 33; RHPL/ Sheila Terry, page 46;
RHPL/Tomlinson, page 14; RHPL/ Adam Woolfitt,
pages 21, 38, 69; Peter Wilson, cover, pages 10, 20, 22,
30, 35, 41, 47, 48, 54, 59, 63, 64, 67, 80, 84, 103, 114;
Zefa, pages 98, 112; Zefa/S. Kube, page 106.
[LF: Life File; RHPL: Robert Harding Picture Library]

Front Cover: Gaudi's La Pedrera, Eixample.
Title Page: Don Quixote addressing the Rambla.

CONTENTS

1
Introducing Barcelona

Vibrant, daring and chic, Barcelona is regarded as Spain's most exciting and cosmopolitan city. Situated on the Mediterranean coast between the long, golden beaches of the **Costa Daurada** to the south and the jagged cliffs and rocky coves of the **Costa Brava** to the north, Barcelona is the capital of **Catalunya**, Spain's most rebellious, independent region. While the city's roots go back over 2000 years to Carthaginian times, Barcelona today is a magnet to progressive thinkers and activists.

Catalunya has provided a stage for expression of all kinds since the late 19th century when Barcelona became the world's centre for extraordinary *modernista* architecture. Great names like Antoni Gaudí have left their legacy of sweeping curves, brilliantly coloured mosaic dragons and twisted chimney stacks on townhouses and parks and the city's most dramatic symbol, the cathedral of the **Sagrada Família**. Legends like **Picasso**, **Miró** and **Dalí** all flourished here, endowing their work to the city's museums, now rich with the cream of 20th-century art.

Barcelona's heart, however, is in the narrow streets of its old **Barri Gòtic** (Gothic quarter), many of the buildings unchanged since medieval times. Twisting passageways overhung with scarlet geraniums in summer give way to elegant old squares, buzzing with life as locals perform their ritual evening stroll, the *passeig*.

High above the city **Montjuïc** hill overlooks many rooftops and spires but the best views are from **Tibidabo** mountain, where the island of Mallorca is visible on a clear day.

TOP ATTRACTIONS

*** **Sagrada Família:** the city's best known landmark and Gaudí's magnificent yet unfinished cathedral.
*** **Miró Foundation:** art gallery packed with the swirls of red, black and green that were the artist's trademark.
*** **Picasso Foundation:** wonderful collection of his paintings and sculptures.
** **The Rambla:** an elegant boulevard bursting with colour from the flower stalls.
** **Eixample:** Barcelona's *modernista* heart.

Opposite: *The Rambla, Barcelona's tree-lined boulevard, is a focal point of the city.*

Above: *The rocky head-land of Montjuïc looms large on Barcelona's shore.*

THE LAND
Mountains and Rivers

Barcelona is located on the narrow coastal plain of Catalunya in the far northeast of Spain, just 149km (93 miles) from the French border. The river **riu Besòs** borders the north, while the rocky headland of Montjuïc to the south forms a natural barrier between the sprawling city and the start of the long, golden beaches of the Costa Daurada.

Catalunya is a mountainous province and the **Serra de Collserola**, a string of wooded hills, the highest point of which is 550m (1805ft) above sea level, provide a green backdrop to the west. The **Mediterranean** forms the eastern border of the city, the busy port area giving way to a stretch of wide, sandy beaches.

The city has several distinctive areas. From the air, the original **Gothic quarter** is a cluster of twisting streets, next to the chequerboard layout of **Eixample**, built in 1860. **Barceloneta**, down by the port and built on a former swamp, has a gridiron pattern of streets while the wealthy suburbs in the hills are green and lush. The entire city is cut in half by the distinctive northwest–southeast boulevard **Avinguda Diagonal**.

BARCELONA FACTFILE
Population of Barcelona: 1,643,542
Metropolitan population: approx. 3,000,000
Total surface area: 99km² (38 sq miles)
Forest and non-urban green areas: 17%
Urban green areas: 9%
Squares and streets: 17%
Length of coastline: 13km (8 miles)
Length of beaches: 5km (3 miles)

Seas and Shores

Barcelona has always been accused of turning its back to the sea and indeed, until the early 1990s, the seafront was derelict and ugly. Massive injections of cash for the Olympic Games in 1992, however, created parks and gardens along the shore. The 5km (3 miles) stretch of sandy beach from the fishing village of Barceloneta to the riu Besòs now has an attractive promenade, with shops, hotels and beach facilities. The outdoor cafés around the Olympic Marina, built specially for the yachting events in 1992, are a popular meeting place.

To the south, the **Costa Daurada**, or gold coast, stretches as far as Tarragona and provides weekend haunts for Barcelona citizens, particularly in summer. Beaches are long, straight and sandy and the area is surprisingly undeveloped. The same could not be said of the **Costa Brava**, 60km (37 miles) to the north, one of the most popular holiday areas of Spain. Beyond the featureless concrete holiday resorts, however, exquisite rocky coves lined with bottle-green pine trees lead all the way to the French border.

Climate

Barcelona enjoys a typical Mediterranean climate of hot summers, mild winters and warm, extended spring and autumn seasons. The latter are the most conducive to wandering round the city, which is ideally suited to exploring on foot.

In July, August and September the daily maximum is usually over 30°C (86°F), although the average is about 23°C (73°F). The air is rarely humid, the city cooled instead by a sea breeze, very refreshing on balmy

ROLLERBLADING

Like most modern cities, Barcelona has a thriving rollerblading culture and on a sunny weekend bladers whizz around the smooth pavements of the new port, the Palau de Mar and the beachfront. When the day trippers have left, the area around the cathedral is a popular haunt and at weekends, skaters head for the Parc de la Ciutadella. You can hire rollerblades for a day from the Edelweiss store on Gran Via and even take lessons and tours. For those who prefer to walk, the tourist board produces a guide called *Walks in Barcelona*.

CLIMATE

Spring and autumn have the most pleasant climates of all the seasons with temperatures in the 20s (centigrade) and cooling breezes from the Mediterranean. July and August are really too hot for most people to enjoy walking round the city although they are still very popular months and the busiest time of year on the Costa Brava to the north and the Costa Daurada to the south. Winter tends to be mild and clear although not generally warm enough to enjoy the outdoor café life that starts in March/April.

BARCELONA	J	F	M	A	M	J	J	A	S	O	N	D
AVERAGE TEMP. °F	50	49	53	53	64	71	74	77	69	60	53	51
AVERAGE TEMP. °C	10	10	11	11	18	22	23	25	20	16	11	11
HOURS OF SUN DAILY	6	5	6	6	7	9	9	9	6	5	4	3
RAINFALL ins.	2	2	2	3	1	1	1	0.5	1	4	2	2
RAINFALL mm	42	42	42	70	25	25	25	10	25	106	42	42
DAYS OF RAINFALL	5	6	6	9	5	4	4	2	5	9	6	6

Below: *Delicious olives are grown all over Spain.*

summer nights when, at weekends, the bars and cafés buzz until dawn. Winter, however, has its advantages. Most days are fresh and bright and the temperature very rarely drops below zero; the average minimum is usually about 7°C (45°F).

March and November are the wettest months, with up to 10 days on which rain falls, while June and July have the most sunshine hours. August can be stifling in the city and is the most popular month for local people to take a long holiday. Visitors, however, can head for one of Barcelona's long, sandy beaches to cool off.

Plant life

Barcelona has just one big park, the Parc de la Ciutadella, site of the Universal Exposition in 1888, with formal gardens, fountains and statues. The city's real green lung is Tibidabo, the highest mountain to the west, cloaked in holm oaks and stone and aleppo pines. Montjuïc is another breathing space, with landscaped gardens and sweeping views of the city. The other parks, Parc Güell and the tiny Parc Joan Miró, for example, are more of a shrine to art and architecture than a celebration of nature but considerable effort has been made to keep native species in the parks, including wild herbs, pines, holm oaks and olives.

Wildlife

With mountains, rivers and coastal plains, Catalunya supports a wide variety of wildlife. The best place for birdwatching is on the seafront, where migratory birds gather. Out of the city, at Montserrat, there is a chance of spotting wild boar, deer, genet cats and martens while further afield, in the Pyrenees, birds of prey and larger mammals are more common.

HISTORY IN BRIEF

The earliest known remains in Catalunya are dolmens or burial chambers, found in the Pyrenees and dating back to 5000BC. By about 700BC it is believed that inhabitants of the mountains had begun to resettle on the coastal plains, mixing with the Iberian race that had migrated from the south of the peninsula. A century later, Greek ships arrived and trading posts were established on what is now the Costa Brava.

Barcino

Around 300BC, Carthaginian troops arrived from what is now Tunisia in North Africa and a small colony, Barcino, was established between the Llobregat and Besòs rivers. **Hannibal**, commander of the Carthaginians, led his troops over the Pyrenees in 214BC to invade Italy, but in the Second Punic War (218–201BC) the Carthaginians were defeated and expelled from Catalunya by the Romans. The **Romans** proceeded to settle the area, making Tarraco, now Tarragona to the south of Barcelona, their capital.

Above: *Magnificent ships like this one in the Maritime Museum are part of Barcelona's heritage.*

Barcino developed into a flourishing trading post, a walled city centred around Mons Taber, the small hill on which the cathedral now stands. The **Plaça de Sant Jaume** was then the forum and is still the political centre of the city today. In 15BC **Emperor Augustus** officially named the city Julia Augusta Favencia Paterna Barcino.

Barcino continued to thrive until around AD300 when its walls had to be fortified against waves of barbarian invasions from northern Europe. In AD476, the **Visigoths** captured the city under King Ataulf, naming their new territory south of the Pyrenees *Gotalonia*.

Moorish Rule

In 711 a new threat, the Moors, a combined force of Arab and Berber armies, swept north from Africa through Spain and in 713 captured Barcino. Their rule was short-

Above: *The Cathedral,*
La Seu, is a brooding mass
in the heart of the city's
Gothic quarter.

lived and in 801 they were forced out
by the **Franks** under the command of
Charlemagne (768–814). The land was
divided up into separate fiefdoms and
after Charlemagne's death, **Guifré el
Pilos** (Wilfred the Hairy) succeeded in
reuniting several of these territories
and appointed himself the first Count
of Barcelona. Before his death in 898
Wilfred had conquered several further
territories including Girona, Besalú
and Montserrat.

In 988, the year which is celebrated
as the birth date of Catalunya, the
ruler Borell II declared Barcelona
an autonomous region. **Ramón
Berenguer I** (1035–76), a subsequent
count, was the first to draw up the
Usatges de Barcelona, a kind of
constitution for the new state.

Significant expansion for Catalunya
came in 1137 thanks to the dynastic marriage of Count
Berenguer IV to Petronilla, heiress to the Kingdom
of Aragón. This union allowed the combined power of
Catalunya and Aragón to expand right across the
Mediterranean, incorporating Naples, Sardinia and much
of southern France. Barcelona's nobility built a series of
magnificent palaces during the 13th century, many of
which are still standing in the Barri Gòtic today.

Under **King Jaume I** (1213–76) Catalunya's first parliament, the **Corts Catalans**, was established and in 1245
Barcelona elected its first governors; their councillors
came to be known as the Consell de Cent and met in the
Generalitat in a chamber which can be visited today.

Ferdinand and Isabella
Catalunya's period of glory, however, came to an end
after the death of the last king, Martin the Humane in
1410, who left no heir. In 1412 a Castilian Prince,
Ferdinand de Antequera, was elected to the throne and

Catalunya rapidly began to be ousted from positions of power. In 1469 Ferdinand's great grandson, also named Ferdinand, married Princess Isabella of Castile, thus uniting Catalunya-Aragón and Castile, Spain's two most powerful territories.

The Catholic Kings, as they were known, drove the last **Moors** out of Spain in 1492 and set upon a religious crusade to root out non-Catholics, during which time the **Jews** of Barcelona and other cities were cruelly persecuted and forced to flee. The persecutions extended to Montserrat which has become the spiritual centre of the Catalan people. In the same year, **Columbus** returned triumphant from the discovery of the New World and Spain's attention began to turn away from the Mediterranean ports to those on the Atlantic. Matters worsened; Barcelona was not allowed to share in the spoils of the new colonies and by 1494, Catalans had been replaced in positions of power by Castilians.

Independent Catalunya

Barcelona became increasingly impoverished until the **Thirty Years' War** with France in 1635, when Catalan

> ### COLUMBUS
>
> Christopher Columbus sailed west from Spain in 1492, hoping to discover a new route to Asia. Instead, he landed on a small island in the Bahamas and went on, over the next five years, to discover **Cuba**, **Jamaica**, **Venezuela**, **Panama** and what is now **Haiti** and the **Dominican Republic**.
>
> Columbus never actually set foot on what is now mainland USA; the closest he got was **Puerto Rico**, although he continues to get the credit for having discovered America. He died in 1506 and was buried in **Seville** in southern Spain before being moved to Santo Domingo and then Havana. In 1899 what was believed to be his remains was returned to Seville, although nobody is quite sure.

HISTORICAL CALENDAR

5000BC Earliest date of burial chambers in the Pyrenees, the mountain range between France and Spain	**1860** Plans for Eixample begin
700BC Mountain dwellers settle on coastal plains	**1914** Catalan provincial government set up
600BC Greek traders establish trading posts	**1923** Successful coup by Primo de Rivera
300BC Barcino established by Carthaginians	**1936** Spanish Civil War begins
15BC Barcino is a thriving Roman city	**1939** Fall of Barcelona
AD476 Visigoths capture the city	**1940s** Catalan language banned under Franco
713 Moors oust Visigoths	**1941** Execution by Franco's troops of Catalan president Lluís Companys
801 Franks expel Moors	**1956** Strikes in Catalunya as economic depression continues
988 Barcelona declared an autonomous region	**1960s** Tourism develops in southern Spain
1245 First Catalan government elected	**1975** Franco dies
1494 Catholic kings replace Catalan government with Castilians	**1979** Catalunya receives a statute of autonomy
1635 Catalan uprising; Catalunya declared autonomous again	**1986** Spain enters European Community
1714 Bourbon King Felipe V takes Barcelona	**1992** Olympic Games in Barcelona
1808 Peninsular War: city rises up against Napoleon	**1996** Coalition conservative government under Prime Minister Jose Maria Aznar.
	2000 Aznar's People's Party re-elected
	2002 Goudí Year

UNUSUAL MUSEUMS

Barcelona has some very unusual museums for those interested in the bizarre. There's a collection of holo- grams at the **Museu d'Holografia** on Plaça Jaume I and the Catalan national coin collection at the **Gabinet Numismàtic de Catalunya** in the Palau de la Virreina. Undertakers' cars and carriages from the last century are displayed at the **Museu de Carrosses Fúnebres** on Sancho de Avila and the **Museu Taurino Gran Via** features heads of famous bulls. Tibidabo, meanwhile, has a collection of robots and mechanical toys in the **Museu d'Autòmates del Tibidabo**.

Below: *Cannons at Montjuïc castle are a reminder of the city's violent past.*

rebels rose up against Castile under the protection of King Louis XIII of France and declared Catalunya an independent Republic. The trade-off was the Treaty of the Pyrenees in 1659, in which Catalunya ceded all its land north of the mountains to **France**.

Independence did not last. In 1714 the Bourbon King, Felipe V, took Barcelona on **September 11**, a day still remembered as a national holiday. A year of bitter siege followed, ending with the Catalan language being banned, the Generalitat abolished and the Ribera district being destroyed in order to make way for a citadel for King Felipe of France.

But in 1808, Catalan sentiment had not faded and the city rose up against **Napoleon** and his army in the Peninsular War. Napoleon and his men were eventually driven out of Spain by the British army. Extensive damage, however, had already been done to Spain's artistic treasures, including the monastery at Montserrat.

Gradual economic recovery followed and Barcelona finally began to share the country's wealth from the American colonies. The city became Spain's centre of technology and the first railway opened in Barcelona in 1848. In 1860 it was decided to accommodate this rapid economic expansion by razing the medieval city walls and constructing a new city, the **Eixample**.

The 20th Century

In 1914, the first Catalan provincial government was set up, only to be crushed by the dictatorship of **General Primo de Rivera**, who carried out a successful military coup in 1923 and remained in power for six years. A second Republic was founded in 1931 and Catalunya was granted limited autonomy under Francesc Macià but unrest was growing all over the country, with strikes and peasant rebellions against a string of land reforms implemented by a succession of rulers.

Spain's problems intensified under the radical right-wing government that came to power in 1934 and proceeded to reverse all the reforms made by the previous government. By 1936, public opinion had swung again and the left took over, but nothing could be done by now to stop Spain sliding into total anarchy. In July of that year, **General Francisco Franco** led an army uprising against the socialist government and all hopes of an independent Catalunya were shattered as the country fell into three years of bitter, bloody civil war between the Republicans and Franco's Nationalists.

Above: *Stone soldiers now guard the fortified walls of Montjuïc.*

The Spanish Civil War (1936 –1939)

During the civil war, Andalucía, Navarra, Galicia and parts of Castilla supported **Franco** but all the major population centres were Republican. The rest of the world was also quick to take sides. Germany and Italy supported Franco, supplying him with troops and munitions. The Soviet Union, meanwhile, called for communists and socialists to unite against fascism. The Republicans received sporadic aid from this brief liaison but Stalin later abandoned the cause.

Over 600,000 lives were lost in bombings, executions, starvation and disease. Horrific bombing raids wiped out entire towns, one such immortalized by Picasso in his famous *Guernica* painting.

Above: *Catalunya is highly political and there's always a demonstration going on somewhere, usually peacefully.*

Eventually, the Republicans were defeated because of in-fighting and sheer lack of resources. The Republican government fled Madrid and took refuge in Barcelona, but by 1938 the Nationalists had begun to advance on Catalunya from all sides.

On 26 January 1939, Franco's troops entered Barcelona. Once again, the Catalan language was banned. Support from Italy and Germany led to Franco's eventual victory in the civil war and in 1939 he proclaimed himself head of state of an exhausted, destitute Spain. **Lluís Companys**, Catalan president of the Generalitat, was executed in Montjuïc in 1941.

Franco's Rule

Even harder times followed, with a mass exodus of Spaniards overseas. A third of a million people fled the country, including artists, scientists and intellectuals, fearful for their lives under Franco, who was busy setting up war tribunals and concentration camps. Thousands of Republicans were imprisoned and execut-ed and any legislation favouring the rights of peasants was revoked. Large numbers of Andalucíans were set-tled in Barcelona to dilute Catalan sentiment. **Censorship** was enforced and by the end of World War II, in which Spain remained neutral, the country was economically and politically isolated. Spain was ostra-cized by the UN and countries cut off diplomatic relations.

Before Franco died in 1975 he handed power over to **King Juan Carlos** who oversaw the transition to democ-racy and is today head of the constitutional monarchy and commander in chief of the armed forces. Spain now comprises 50 provinces in 17 autonomous regions; **Catalunya**, for example, is an autonomous region, the capital of which is **Barcelona**.

A TASTE OF ANDALUCIA

Barcelona has a surprisingly large Andalucían population and consequently enjoys more than its fair share of flamenco festivals and events. In April, the *Feria de Abril* at Barbará de Vallés just outside the city hosts some talented perform-ers while the *Caixa* Flamenco Festival in the city in June attracts some big acts from Andalucía. There are also regular performances at the *tablao* (flamenco club) at the Poble Espanol, although some of these are rather touristy.

GOVERNMENT AND ECONOMY

In 1979 Catalunya finally received its statute of autonomy and Catalan was recognized as the official language. In 1982 the **Socialist Workers' Party** (PSOE), led by Felipe Gonzales, was elected. The Socialist government successfully integrated Spain into the European Community in 1986 and the country continued to recover economically, putting itself in the world spotlight in 1992 with the **Expo** in Seville, the **Olympics** in Barcelona and **European City of Culture** in Madrid all falling in the same year. Since 1996, the centre-right Jose Maria Aznar has been Prime Minister, having been re-elected in 2000's general election.

The Olympics was the catalyst for over $2 billion of joint ventures between the public and private sectors. The inner city was renovated; new roads and highways were built, including a four lane ring road; and the port and rail links were upgraded. In a mission to shift Barcelona from secondary industry into the service sector, then mayor Pasqual Maragall encouraged heavy industry to move to the Zona Franca, the area between Montjuic and the airport. Two new business districts were created: the Carre Tarragona, location of car manufacturer SEAT's headquarters; and around the World Trade Centre on the seafront.

The service sector now employs some 50% of the working population in areas like banking, finance, tourism and insurance, although SEAT is still one of the whole country's largest employers.

CHILDREN IN BARCELONA

Barcelona has a surprising amount to offer children, not least two permanent funfairs, one on the hill of Montjuïc and one on Tibidabo. There are all sorts of rides around the city, too, from the vintage tram at **Tibidabo** to the cable car across the harbour. The Science Museum is a 'hands-on' attraction with lots of buttons to press; the aquarium and **Imax** cinema at the new **Maremagnum Centre** are ideal for a rainy day. Kids also enjoy the labyrinth at **Horta** and the football museum at **Camp Nou** and for an introduction to arts and crafts, try the **Poble Espanyol** on Montjuïc. The biggest treat, however, is a day at **Port Aventura**, Spain's answer to Disney, an hour or so to the south of the city.

Left: *Spain's royal family is highly respected.*

Opposite: *Most people in Barcelona speak Catalan and Castilian Spanish.*
Below: *Petanca is highly popular among the older generation.*

THE PEOPLE

Catalans see themselves as mid-European rather than Spanish and given the choice, would be totally independent from Spain. Sometimes you may hear Catalunya referred to, by Catalans at least, as a country rather than an autonomous region of Spain.

Catalan people are known to be hard working and friendly and a strong service ethic is evolving as the city moves into the tertiary industry. Fierce rivalry, however, exists between Barcelona and Madrid, the capital, in everything from grants of public money, to which has the better football team. Old resentments run deep, too; the Andalucíans who were relocated to Barcelona under Franco's rule, to dilute Catalan spirit, are generally looked down on and tend to have jobs inferior to those of Catalans. Barcelona, like other Spanish cities, has a small gypsy population which is generally not integrated into mainstream society.

Visitors to Catalunya may be surprised at the almost complete absence of Spanish clichés like bullfighting. This sport, which is attended by many tourists in the summer, is supported more in the south and in Madrid. In Barcelona, the obsession is with football. The team, FC Barcelona, enjoys hero status. Matches at the mighty

Camp Nou stadium are always a sell-out and the atmosphere on the Rambla after a victory is electric with the honking of car horns and the popping of *cava* corks.

Barcelona is a genuinely cosmopolitan city and political expression is rife, with frequent, usually peaceful demonstrations. The city has a strong feminist movement as well as a thriving gay community which migrates to the beach resort of Sitges to the south in summer.

Language

For over 1000 years, **Catalan**, a combination of Spanish, Latin and medieval French, has been spoken in Catalunya. The language in 12th-century Catalunya was almost identical to the *langue d'oc* which was spoken on the other side of the Pyrenees and quickly became the common trading language of the Mediterranean.

Catalan is still very widespread, more so than it would seem and is also spoken in parts of Aragón, Andorra, parts of the Pyrenees and even southern Italy. The dialects of the Balearic islands today are variations of Catalan rather than Castilian Spanish. The language looks strange to read and is not particularly easy to pronounce with its harsh, guttural sounds but it can be mastered with some knowledge of French.

Throughout history, however, there have been attempts to suppress Catalan, most recently during Franco's dictatorship, in which books in Catalan were burned, and the language itself was banned on TV, the radio, in the press and was no longer taught in the schools. Catalan culture went underground for the second time and their leader, Josep Tarradellas, was exiled.

Now, however, following a strong revival, Catalan has all but taken over from Castilian in Barcelona. Road signs, maps and advertising hoardings are all in Catalan. The language is spoken in offices, taxis and shops and in over 50% of households. Almost everybody, however, is bilingual and visitors will always get by in Castilian.

CATALAN PRONUNCIATION

Catalan is mystifying to anyone who has just mastered basic Spanish as it's completely different, even though some words have a similar root. Here are a few of the more peculiar pronunciations:
g followed by **e** or **i** is pronounced like *zh* in Zhivago
ig is pronounced like *tch* in hatch
n before **f** or **v** is sometimes pronounced *m*
r is rolled at the beginning of a word and usually silent at the end
v at the beginning of a word is pronounced *b* and *f* elsewhere
w is pronounced either *v* or *b*
x is pronounced *sh* in most words

Above: *Residents of Gràcia admire the entries for an art competition.*

Religion

Roman Catholicism is the dominant faith in Spain although there is no state religion. Small pockets of Protestantism exist and Barcelona also has a synagogue in Gràcia and two mosques in the centre.

The Arts

Barcelona is an art lover's paradise, with some of the best modern collections in Europe and the magnificent medieval section in the **Museu Nacional d'Art de Catalunya** (MNAC) on Montjuïc. There are museums of graphic art, decorative art, ceramic art, contemporary art and textiles but again, like its architecture, it is the city's 20th-century work that fascinates visitors so much. The centre of the artistic community in the early 20th century was undoubtedly **Els Quatre Gats**, a bar to the north of the Barri Gòtic where **Picasso**, **Ramón Casa** and **Pere Romeu** formed the nucleus of the crowd.

Art in Catalunya and all over Spain was suppressed during the civil war, when the country experienced a tremendous drain of talent, but later this century, dedicated museums were opened to showcase the work of **Pablo Picasso**, **Antoni Tàpies** and **Joan Miró**. In Figueres, a couple of hours' drive to the north, the great surrealist **Salvador Dalí** opened a collection of his own in 1974.

GAY BARCELONA

Barcelona is a liberal and cosmopolitan city with a big gay population, much of which moves to the coastal resort of Sitges for weekends during the summer season. There are bars, clubs and hotels favoured by gays and several events throughout the year, including a gay pride march on 28 June. Information can be obtained from **SexTienda**, the gay shop on carrer Rauric in the Barri Gòtic, or Zeus on carrer Riera Alta. The weekly listings guide, *Guia del Ocio*, also features gay clubs and events. Outside the city, however, the conservative country villages tend to be less tolerant of gay society.

New museums continue to open in Barcelona today. After extensive renovations, the MNAC on Montjuïc has opened more rooms, and in 1996 a brand new museum opened in the Raval quarter, the **Museu d'Art Contemporani de Barcelona**, containing work by Klee and Calder, among others. And for amateur shoppers, some excellent local talent is displayed every Sunday at the market in Plaça Sant Josep Oriol.

Architecture

Until the city walls were pulled down in the middle of the last century, there was little opportunity to expand Barcelona and all architectural gems from before that time are confined to the **Barri Gòtic**, such as the cathedral, the medieval palaces around the **Plaça del Rei** and the church of **Santa María del Mar**. But while Barcelona contains many fine examples of Gothic, Romanesque and Baroque architecture, it is the *modernista* work that people flock to see. This developed in the early 20th century as architects began to experiment with new curves and floral ornamentation on everything from the roof of a building to its iron balconies and stained glass windows.

Leading architects are employed today to design the city's street furniture as part of a clever initiative by the Department of Urban Elements, maintaining Barcelona's reputation as a fashionable, forward-thinking metropolis.

Left: *Twisted chimney stacks are typical of Gaudí's style.*

MODERNISTA SHOPS

Pharmacies were particularly receptive to *modernista* design and some elaborate examples remain today. Look out for the Farmácia J de Bolós on carrer de València with its elaborate stained glass windows, (one featuring an orange tree), ornate lamps, decorated ceilings and cabinets full of old, decorated jars. Bakeries, too, seemed to enjoy elaborate façades and the Antigua Casa Figueras on the Rambla is one of the most remarkable ones, recently restored to its former glory of stained glass and with a brightly coloured mosaic design.

BEST BUYS

- Spanish ceramics.
- Art books and posters from the museum shops.
- Design items from Vinçon – popular interior shop.
- Designer clothes from the Boulevard Rosa mall on Passeig de Gràcia.
- Leather shoes for men and women.
- Torró Catalan almond fudge.
- Quince jelly.
- Catalan honey.
- Spicy sausages to take home (well wrapped) from La Boquería market.
- Cava (Spanish champagne).

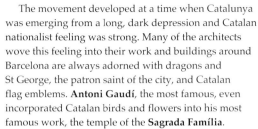

LLUÍS DOMÈNECH I MONTANER (1850-1923)

Domènech i Montaner quali-
fied as an architect at the age
of 23 and later taught at
Barcelona's architectural col-
lege. He was an active
member of the Catalan
nationalist movement. Much
of the beauty of his work can
be attributed to other sculptors and artists but his skill lay
in new construction tech-
niques blended with these
decorative effects; look at the
intricate tiled effect of the
Palau de la Música Catalana
and the Mudéjar-inspired
Hospital de Sant Pau, its
clean diagonal lines a rebel-
lion against the chequerboard
pattern of the Eixample.

The movement developed at a time when Catalunya was emerging from a long, dark depression and Catalan nationalist feeling was strong. Many of the architects wove this feeling into their work and buildings around Barcelona are always adorned with dragons and St George, the patron saint of the city, and Catalan flag emblems. **Antoni Gaudí**, the most famous, even incorporated Catalan birds and flowers into his most famous work, the temple of the **Sagrada Família**.

Most of the major works are in Barcelona, which has 2000 listed buildings, although regional towns have their share of gems. Look out for pavement designs, lamp-posts and benches as well as houses, or the occasional splash of colour in a brilliant stained glass window.

The most famous buildings in the city are the **Mansana de la Discòrdia**, three fantastical houses on the Passeig de Gràcia; **La Pedrera**, Gaudí's wavy apartment block, located on the same boulevard; Gaudí's bizarre **Sagrada Família**; Domènech i Montaner's magnificent

concert hall, the **Palau de la Música Catalana**; his **Castell dels Tres Dragons** and the extraordinary, tiled **Hospital de Sant Pau**. But many, many more are dotted around the Eixample.

Also not to be missed is Gaudí's **Parc Güell** in Gràcia, what was supposed to be an entire *modernista* housing complex but today serves as one of the city's most beautiful green oases.

Further developments in architecture did not happen until the second revival of the century, a huge facelift for the 1992 Olympic Games. Graceful buildings with clean lines, sheer glass and metal façades were constructed, such as the Japanese-designed sports arena, the **Palau Sant Jordi** on Montjuïc and the two towers overlooking the **Olympic Marina**. Post-modernist parks also sprung up, such as the

Left: *Intricate tiling covers the stonework in Gaudí's Parc Güell.*
Opposite: *Parc Güell is just one collection of Gaudí's bizarre designs.*

Parc de l'Espanya Industrial near Central-Sants station, trying to make modern art an integral part of the city. Along the same theme of light, space and simplicity is the **Fundació Joan Miró** on Montjuïc and the new **Museu d'Art Contemporani de Catalunya**, designed by American architect Richard Weir.

Antoni Gaudí (1852–1926)

Barcelona's most famous son, Antoni Gaudí was sponsored from an early age by the wealthy Güell family, hence the names of many of his buildings – Palau Güell, Finca Güell and Parc Güell, for example. His earlier works, the Casa Milà and Casa Batlló, were expressionist with their undulating form and face-like features, but as religion played an important role in his life Gaudí's designs, principally the Sagrada Família on which he worked from 1883 until his death in 1926, contained more religious symbolism. Nature, with its flowing lines and organic shapes, also had a tremendous influence on Gaudí's work. Sadly, in 1926, by which time he had become almost a recluse, living alone on the building site of the Sagrada Família, he was run over by a tram. Nobody recognized the tattered old man but when his identity became clear, the streets of Barcelona were packed for his funeral. 2002, the 150th anniversary of his birth, has been designated 'Gaudí Year' in the city.

DESIGNER TOMBS

So popular and so fashionable was *modernista* that land had to be found for a new cemetery so that the upper classes could have space for specially commissioned, elaborate tombs. The southeast face of Montjuïc was chosen and the miniature temples and palaces are visible today from the new ring road that leads to the airport. Josep Villaseca built a tomb for the Batlló family guarded by Egyptian-style angels, while Puig constructed mini-masterpieces for the Terrades family (who commissioned the turreted Casa de les Punxes) and the Barons of Quadres, whose former home on the Diagonal now houses the Museu de la Música.

Above: *All kinds of music, from jazz to classical, are performed in Barcelona.*
Opposite above: *The Olympic Games in 1992 have inspired city dwellers to keep fit.*

JOSEP PUIG I CADAFALCH (1867–1957)

An art historian and politician, Puig was a disciple of Domènech i Montaner, although his work was more Gothic in style with lots of detailed floral decoration and some dramatic medieval influences, like the towers and turrets of the Casa Punxes on the Diagonal. One of his most-visited works is Els Quatre Gats, the café in the Barri Gòtic where Picasso and his contemporaries would drink.

Also a Catalan nationalist, Puig was president from 1916 to 1923 of the Catalan regional government.

Music

Barcelona has some of the best nightlife in Spain and is a wonderful place in which to enjoy live music from **jazz** in smoky basement bars to exuberant **Latin American**, where people dance on the tables. Folk music is growing in popularity and its most famous expression today is in the **Sardana**, the national dance of Catalunya, performed on Sunday in front of the cathedral.

An experience not to be missed is a classical concert in the stunning, modern **Palau de la Música**, all ornate sculpture and magnificent stained glass. Likewise the opera in the new Liceu, which promises to be one of Europe's most spectacular opera houses, where you may be lucky enough to see a performance by the legendary soprano **Montserrat Caballe**, Catalunya's most famous daughter.

Open air music on a lovely hot summer's night is always magical and the **Teatre Grec** on Montjuïc couldn't be a more beautiful setting, among scented, subtropical gardens, the city lights glittering far down below. Or you could try the **Saló de Tinell** (the place where the Spanish Inquisition once sat), the Gothic hall of the Palau Reial in the old centre (Barri Gòtic), where free recitals often take place. A variety of exhibitions and other events are also held in this lofty, handsome hall.

Sport and Recreation

The Olympic Games did wonders for sport in the city, with world class facilities being developed for athletics, sailing, track cycling and swimming. There are also facilities for tennis, polo, horse riding, roller and ice skating and squash. At the new marina, visitors can take sailing lessons, rent a windsurfer or kayak and even learn scuba diving.

Outside the city and up and down the coast are several excellent golf clubs which accept temporary members.

Football, of course, is a national passion and while visitors are unlikely to play, attending a match at the Camp Nou stadium is to sample Barcelona at its most passionate. Cycling is a rather popular sport and at weekends, country roads are packed with crowds of colourful, lycra-clad racers. Further afield, the Pyrenees and their foothills present all sorts of opportunities for hiking, climbing, canoeing, white water rafting and, in winter, skiing.

FLAMENCO

Though not an especially Catalan phenomenon, flamenco is performed in a number of clubs around the city.

Essentially an outlet for passion and unhappiness, good flamenco is a kind of spiritual bond between musicians, dancer and onlookers, as the raw emotion of the song, the hypnotic hand-clapping and finger-snapping of the audience and the fantastically fast stamping of the dancer build up into a cathartic finale, often accompanied by spontaneous shouts of encouragement and emotion.

Strands of many cultures have come together to form the music as we know it today, but it originates from the gypsies of Seville, Jerez and Cadiz in the 19th century, who sang mournful laments of lost love and oppression.

Below: *FC Barcelona is one of Spain's top football teams.*

GAMBLING

There are three casinos within striking distance of the city, although none in the city itself. The first, **Gran Casino de Barcelona** at Sant Pere de Ribes, a town near Sitges on the Costa Daurada, is housed in a mansion and has a nightclub as well as the usual gaming rooms. The **Casino de Perelada** in the Empordà region is situated in an old castle and a third, the glitzy **Lloret de Mar casino** in the modern holiday resort on the Costa Brava is more modern. For less effort, play the Spanish lottery, which sells tickets at booths throughout the city.

Below: *Every Sunday, locals gather at the cathedral to dance the Sardana.*

Festivals

Catalan festivals are exuberant affairs, the streets decked with bunting, red and yellow Catalan flags fluttering in the breeze, bands playing and people dancing in the streets. Festivals take place for all kinds of reasons – national holidays, saints' days or pagan rituals.

Every village has a saint's day and to participate in the celebrations gives a true insight into Catalan culture. The whole village turns out to parade behind an effigy of the saint with much drinking and dancing as the procession winds its way out to the countryside for huge picnics and more merrymaking.

Certain sights are unique to Barcelona. On 23 April, **St George's Day**, the patron saint of Catalunya is celebrated with gusto. Everybody dresses as a devil or an animal and parades noisily through the streets, letting off firecrackers. On 24 September, **La Mercé**, the main festival of the city's calendar, *gegants*, giant papier-mâché figures in brilliant colours are marched through the city to the **Plaça de Sant Jaume**. At the same time, huge human towers, or *castells*, are built up to 10m (33ft) high, the challenge being for a young boy to climb to the top. The night sky is ablaze with fireworks and live bands play in every square.

NIGHTLIFE

Barcelona comes alive after dark and buzzes until dawn. There's a lot to choose from: live jazz, classical, funfairs, discos, flamenco shows and endless bars.

Everything happens late in Spain and Barcelona is no exception. Go for a stroll at sunset, nibble a few tapas and enjoy a sherry or a gin and tonic. Then move on to a restaurant at around 22:00. After dinner, many people go to another bar before repairing to a disco or *discoteca* around midnight. Some of these stay open until 06:00. You need stamina for this city!

The Rambla and Barri Gòtic

Plaça del Pi and the Plaça Reial are the most atmospheric places on a summer night with outdoor seating. There are some good bars in the Barri Xines, best sought out with a local, and along the Passeig de Born. Try Ample and Mercé, two streets forming the southern border of the Barri Gòtic, for authentic bars where wine is poured from barrels and free tapas are sometimes handed out.

Eixample and Gràcia

By far the most fashionable area, with a string of designer tapas bars along the Passeig de Gràcia. All the best discos, often with startling decor and beautiful people to match, are here and needless to say, the prices match the venues.

Above: *'Designer' tapas are a feature of the non-stop Barcelona nightlife.*

THE PASSEIG

The *passeig* – an evening walk or stroll – is an essential component of Barcelona nightlife in the summer months. When offices have closed, locals slowly parade the city's trendiest areas, stopping for tapas and to greet friends. A second *passeig* takes place between tapas and dinner, usually around 23:00, after which most people repair to a bar and then a nightclub.
The best locations for people-watching are the Rambla, packed with outdoor bars and cafés; on Montjuïc to watch the sunset; Plaça del Pi in the Barri Gòtic; and the Gran Via de les Corts Catalanes. One of the newer areas for outdoor drinking is the Moll de la Fusta, the seafront by the Barri Gòtic, developed as part of the city's facelift for the Olympic Games.

Along the Waterfront

Many of the good fish restaurants in the old fishing village of Barceloneta have been moved to a trendy warehouse conversion, Palau de Mar, becoming fashionable tapas bars in the process. Further north, the Olympic Marina buzzes with life in summer with over 50 bars and restaurants overlooking the yacht basin.

Also worth a visit is **Montjuïc**, where the bars around the Poble Espanyol get very lively in summer and there's an exceptionally popular club, Torre de Avila, with moving walls and transparent floors.

Above: *Catalan cuisine does wonderful things with seafood.*
Opposite: *Can Culleretes is Barcelona's oldest restaurant, specializing in Catalan dishes.*

FOOD AND DRINK

Catalan food is influenced by cultures from all over the Mediterranean and incorporates pasta from Italy, rice from Byzantine times and rich sauces from France. Food has two broad bases: wholesome peasant fare of sausage, pork and dripping on one hand and exquisite seafood from the Mediterranean on the other such as squid, clams, king prawns, delicious crispy fried anchovies and salt cod.

Expect plenty of rich sauces, thick fish stews and mouthwatering paella, giant prawns and chicken pieces nesting on aromatic saffron rice. While paella originated in Valencia, Catalunya has adopted the dish and varieties are available in specialist restaurants.

Most restaurants offer *pa am tomáquet* as a starter, slices of crusty bread rubbed with tomatoes and olive oil. Other starters include a mixture of nuts, pulses, meat and fish; *faves la Catalana*, for example, is stewed beans with slices of spicy sausage, while *canelons* is pasta with meat and a white sauce. Vegetarians will do better with starters than main courses; worth trying are *espinacs a la Catalana*, spinach with pine nuts and raisins, and *samfiana*, a tasty hotpot of onions, peppers, aubergine and tomatoes.

COFFEE

Good, strong espresso-style coffee is normally drunk in Barcelona but there are plenty of alternatives. *Cafe con leche* is made with hot milk, while cappuccino is frothy. *Cafe cortado* is espresso with cold milk. Nescafé invariably means a sachet of decaf. Liqueur coffees are often drunk after meals (and occasionally with breakfast). Try the Café Roma on Plaça d'Angel for an almost bewildering choice.

In main courses, fish and chicken are often mixed, for example, as in a paella. Try *llagosta amb pollastre*, lobster in a rich sauce with chicken. Squid in its own ink is very popular, as is *arros negre*, rice cooked with squid ink. Fish and shellfish are often grilled (*a la plancha*) or steamed (*a la marinera*) with sauce on the side, either *allioli*, a kind of mayonnaise with garlic, or *romesco*, a spicy tomato sauce from Tarragona. Meat dishes include *conill*, or rabbit; *mongetes amb botifarra*, roast pork sausage with beans that have been cooked in pork dripping, and *escudella de pagès*, a vegetable and meat stew.

Vegetables are not taken particularly seriously, especially as a main course, but there are some very typical, very tasty salads available. *Escalivada* is a simple aubergine, pepper and onion salad, while *esqueixada* is a green salad with olives, tomato and *bacalao* (salt cod) added. *Xato* is a special salad from Sitges, south of the city, featuring anchovies, olives and *bacalao*.

Catalan people have something of a sweet tooth and a dessert not to be missed is *crema Catalana*, a delicious creamy custard of eggs, milk and sugar with a crunchy caramelized crust. Otherwise, try rice pudding (*arros amb llet*), *postres de músic*, a kind of fruit cake, or *mel i mató*, curd cheese with honey. Look out for *xocolateries*, particularly in the Barri Gòtic, tiny hole-in-the-wall confectionery shops selling freshly-made chocolate truffles and almond and nougat delicacies.

Of course, cuisine from all over Spain is available in Barcelona. Try the fresh mountain trout stuffed with ham from Andalucía; seafood pies from Galicia, and *chorizo* and *cocido* – sausages and meat with chickpeas from Castile; even part-

> ### VEGETARIAN SURVIVAL
>
> Vegetarianism is not widely appreciated by the meat-eating Catalans but there are a few things to choose from on the menu. Useful phrases include: *Sóc vegetariàna* or *Non puc menjar carn* (I can't eat meat). There are plenty of pizza restaurants in town as well as Indian and Chinese, and a handful of vegetarian restaurants, all of which serve vegetarian options. Self Naturista on carrer Santa Ana is popular with a changing daily menu and lots of salads, while Illa de Gràcia in Gràcia, carrer Sant Domènech 19, serves pasta, rice, crepes and salads.

Tapas are usually displayed
under a glass case at the bar
so you can point out your
selection, but it always helps
to interpret the menu. Menus
are presented in Castilian and
Catalan and the following are
tapas typical of the area:
Albóndigas: meatballs
in sauce.
Anchoas (Catalan *anxoves*):
anchovies.
Boquerones: fresh anchovies
fried in a light batter,
highly recommended.
Caracoles: snails, usually
in a spicy sauce.
Chorizo: spicy sausage.
Croqueta: fish or
chicken croquets.
Gambas: shrimp.
Mejillones: mussels.
Patatas bravas: sautéed
potatoes in a spicy sauce
Tortilla (Catalan *truita*):
Spanish omelette.

ridge in chocolate from Navarra.

Snacks

While hotels offer buffet breakfasts, locals tend to
stick to coffee with croissants or doughnuts (*churros*).
Torrades, alternatively, are toasted rolls and some
places serve *truita*, cold tortilla for breakfast.

At lunchtime, plenty of establishments serve sand-
wiches in long, crispy baguettes. While the Spanish
tradition is for three hour lunches, the reality is that
most office workers in Barcelona have to grab a quick
snack just like those in other cities around the world.

Tapas

Something that no visitor should miss is *tapas*,
mini-portions of snacks on display at the bar in many
restaurants. Tapas tend to be served with cocktail sticks
and could be anything from a plate of cheese to a few
slices of salami or *chorizo*. The term actually means
'lid' in Castilian Spanish and originates from the small
dishes of nuts or olives that bartenders would place
over a glass earlier this century, apparently to keep the
flies out. Simple tapas used to be free but have evolved
into such a bar culture that almost everywhere charges for them now.
Nonetheless, a few dishes shared between
a group of friends is a
fun and cost effective way to eat. Simply
point at what you want – try garlic fried
mushrooms (*champinones*), croquets of
fish or chicken, steamed fresh mussels
with diced tomatoes (*mejillones*) and
delicious sautéed potatoes with chilli
sauce (*patatas bravas*). Real tapas special-
ists may have 30 different dishes on
display, including some Catalan specialities. Look out for *chipirones* (whole baby
squid), *pulpo* (octopus), *caracoles* (snails in
a spicy sauce) and *habas con jamon* (broad
beans with ham). For a larger portion,
ask for a *racion*. The idea, though, is to

wander from bar to bar trying a few
tapas in each.

What to drink

There are several wine-producing areas just outside
Barcelona, the best known of which is **Penedès**, where
the Torres family makes the famous Vina Sol and the
Freixenet and **Codorniu** houses produce award-winning
cava, or sparkling wine. The *brut* or *brut nature* bears the
closest resemblance to French champagne. Reds are produced around **Tarragona** and **Priorat**, to the south, while
more whites come from **Conca de Barberá**.

Wine is grown all over Spain and the most famous
are probably the *riojas* (light aromatic reds) from the
north and the wines from **Navarra**, mainly rosés and
heavier reds. Both wine and *cava* are served by the glass
in many tapas bars and in the city's *xampanyerías*, bars
of varying quality specializing in sparkling wine or *cava*.
Be warned: a *xampanyería* could mean 20 vintages lined
up behind the bar or in the case of Xampanyet, one of
the most famous, semi-sweet fizz from unlabelled litre
bottles with replaceable corks!

Beer in Barcelona is the same as anywhere else in
Spain, the two most popular brands being **San Miguel**
and **Estrella**. **Sangría** is served on feast days, a lethal con-
coction of red wine, lemonade, fruit and brandy which
slides down all too easily on a hot summer night. Bars in
Barcelona specialize in different types of drink. As well as
the *xampanyería* there's a *cervecería* serving mainly beer,
or a *cocktelería* serving spirits, as its name implies.

Above: *Miles of cool* cava
*cellars make an interesting
day trip from Barcelona.*
Opposite: *Wine merchants
in Catalunya stock a tremendous variety to take home.*

XAMAPANYERIAS

A few bars in the city specialize in *cava*, the sparkling
wine produced in the
Penedès region outside the
metropolitan area. There are,
however, different interpretations of a champagne bar.
Some have 30 or more varieties lined up behind the bar
for tasting while others sell
only one, served in unlabelled
bottles at rock bottom prices.
The Xampanyet in carrer
Montcada, close to the
Picasso Museum, sells wine
that is semi-sweet and rather
low grade, but the bar
remains popular with the
locals. Elsewhere, bars serving still wine will usually serve
cava by the glass at reasonable prices.

2
La Rambla

Barcelona is a city where people walk, or rather stroll and there is no better place to start than the **Rambla**, a long, straight promenade stretching from the busy Plaça de Catalunya to the seafront. This is Barcelona in microcosm; one of colour, life, street performers, majestic buildings and political demonstrations.

In the 13th century, the Rambla (which comes from the Arabic 'Ramla', or torrent) was a seasonal stream running outside the city walls. When the walls had to be enlarged and rebuilt, the stream, which was used as a road in the long hot summers, was incorporated. From the 15th to the 17th century, several palaces and academic institutions were built here. In the 18th century, the Rambles, or Rambla, was recognized as a promenade and lined with trees.

There are, in fact, five Rambles. Heading south from the Plaça de Catalunya is the **Rambla de Canaletes**, which is lined with bookstalls and named after an old fountain. The **Rambla dels Estudis** is where bird sellers gather and was once the site of Barcelona's first university. The most colourful, **Rambla dels Flors**, is packed with flower stalls of every colour and description. Next, the **Rambla dels Caputxins** passes the **Teatre del Liceu** opera house and on the other side, one of the city's most beautiful, hidden squares, the **Plaça del Pi**. This Rambla also bisects the city's dubious neighbourhood, the **Barri Xines**. Finally, the broad sweep of the **Rambla Santa Monica** opens out onto the Mediterranean, a 50m (164ft) monument to Columbus marking the end of the promenade.

DON'T MISS

*** Rambla dels Flors: colourful flower stalls line the promenade.
*** La Boquería: Barcelona's biggest and best market.
** Palau Güell: an early work by Gaudí, built as a palace for his patron, Eusebio Güell.
** Museu d'Art Contemporani: Barcelona's newest modern art museum with works by Miró and Klee.
** Plaça del Pi: beautiful, shady square.

Opposite: *Plaça de Catalunya is a popular picnic spot in summer.*

La Rambla

(Map labels:)
Plaça de Catalunya
C. d'Elisabets
LE MERIDIEN
BARCELONA (H)
Pintor Fortuny
C. del Carme
Església de Betlem
Palau de la Virreina
Plaça de la Gardunya
Mercat la Boqueria
C. de Hospital
Barri Xines
LAS FLORES
Liceu
Plaça de Boqueria
C. Sant Pau
Teatre del Liceu
ESPAÑA
C. de la Unió
ORIENTE
C. Nou de la Rambla
Palau Güell
C. de l'Art del Teatre
Plaça del Teatre
Drassanes
Museu de Cera
Plaça Portal de la Pau
Monument a Colom
CENT SANTA ANNA
RIVOLI RAMBLAS
Plaça Vila de Madrid
Palau Moja
C. PORTAFERRISSA
Església de Santa Maria del Pi
Plaça del Pi
Plaça Sant Josep Oriol
C. DE FERRAN
RIALTO (H)
C. Lleona
Plaça Reial
C. dels Escudellers
C. Josep Anselm Clavé
Passeig de Colom
Cinturó del Litoral
100 m
100 yd

WALKING THE RAMBLA

The best time to walk the Rambla is at the weekend, when most of Barcelona turns out for a leisurely stroll, or on balmy summer evenings as people perform their nightly *passeig* before settling outside a bar for tapas and a cold beer.

Plaça de Catalunya ★

This vast square is the geographical centre of the city, between the tangled alleys of the **Barri Gòtic** (Gothic quarter) and the wide, elegant boulevards of the **Eixample** to the north. Deck chairs, lawns and fountains adorn the middle of the square, often packed with people lounging on the grass, reading the newspaper. The Café Zurich on the corner is a popular stop for morning coffee and people-watching, although a vantage point on the terrace carries a premium for drinks.

Rambla de Canaletes ★

Heading south from the Plaça de Catalunya, this boulevard is named after an old iron drinking fountain. Drink from here, the legend says, and you will always return to Barcelona. Bookstalls and newspaper stands line the street, selling Spanish and international titles, new and second-hand. Sundry political groups set up tables here, draped with banners and slogans. When there's a big football match on, the atmosphere is electric, with car horns hooting and people cheering.

MEDIA

Foreign newspapers can be found among the Rambla's many bookstalls. Local papers are of a high standard if you read Spanish. The *El Periodico* publication (in Castilian) is a combination of serious news coverage and large splashes of photo-journalism.
Catalan speakers have two papers: *Avui* and *El Diari de Barcelona*. The *Guia del Ocio*, the weekly listings guide, is the most useful 'what's on' reference.

Rambla dels Estudis **

The incessant chirping of caged songbirds has given this Rambla the nickname '**Rambla dels Ocells**' (of the birds). Just about anything with fur, scales or feathers is on sale at the street stalls here: hamsters, rabbits, macaws, cockatoos, budgerigars, even tortoises and fish. On the right hand side, the Església de Betlem is a former Jesuit church,

built in 1681 but destroyed inside during the Spanish Civil War. On the opposite side, the **Palau Moja** was built in the 18th century and more recently restored by the city's cultural department. The main hall inside contains murals by Francesc Pla and is used occasionally for exhibitions. In 1714, Barcelona's first university stood on this site, although the academic establishments today are dotted all over the city.

At the end of this section of the promenade, the graceful, Rococo building on the right is the **Palau de la Virreina** which today houses the cultural services of the city council. The equestrian statues which flank the façade are by Gargallo. Exhibitions are held here throughout the year; check with the tourist board for details of opening times.

Mercat Sant Josep **

A tall, iron gate on the right of the Rambla marks the entrance to **La Boquería**, Barcelona's biggest and best known market. Built between 1840 and 1870, this cavernous hall resembles a railway station and is a hive of activity from dawn, as stallholders set up in competition with one another. Brilliantly coloured piles of vegetables and fruit, tables stacked high with pungent cheeses and long strings of plump, spicy sausages make the market a wonderful place to browse around, not to mention displays of glistening fish, fresh from the morning's catch. Open 08:00–19:00, Monday–Saturday.

Above: *La Boquería is Barcelona's best source of fresh produce.*
Opposite: *The Rambla is always buzzing with life as locals and tourists stroll in the fresh air.*

MARKETS

Barcelona has some fascinating markets, all worth a visit. **La Boquería** on the Rambla is the biggest food market and practically a work of art, so spectacular is its architecture. The lovely Plaça del Pi off the Rambla has an antique market on a Thursday and a honey market on the first Friday and Saturday of the month while the neighbouring Plaça Sant Josep Oriol has an art market every weekend. Coins and stamps are traded every Sunday in the Plaça Reial and along the Rambla, you can buy birds, flowers and animals. There's a better craft market in Gràcia on the first Sunday of the month in Avinguda Pau Casals.

Shopping in markets in Barcelona is part of the city's culture and everyone from professional chefs to office workers frequents La Boquería. When the market opens at 08:00, people congregate around the Bar Pinocho inside, although there are plenty of other stand-up snack and tapas bars in here.

Above: *Rain or shine, buskers and performers entertain the crowds on the Rambla.*

Rambla dels Flors ★★★

The most beautiful of the Rambla, this section of the boulevard is lined with exotic flower stalls, huge bunches of cut flowers in buckets, clashing brilliantly with one another in a riot of orange, pink, scarlet and electric blue. You can buy anything from a pet Venus flytrap to a Bonsai tree or a cactus garden in a jar.

This section of the Rambla also has some wonderful sights and while it's tempting to lose oneself in the scents and colours of the flowers, a glance upwards reveals an artist's easel on a wrought iron balcony, or a dusky pink-coloured façade with faded frescoes. Look down a side street and you'll see a clown painting his face with a mournful smile, while buskers play haunting melodies on pan pipes and jugglers entertain the crowd.

TELEVISION

Almost every bar has a television, invariably blaring out a football match. The two national channels are TV1 and La 2, while TV3 and Canal 33 are in Catalan. Antena 3 and Tele 5 are private channels. Unless you're a football fan, Spanish television is not really particularly exciting, consisting largely of recycled overseas soaps and boisterous game shows. The smart hotels all have satellite, picking up Eurosport, CNN and various English-language cable channels.

Casa Bruno Quadros ★

The end of this pretty Rambla is marked by an amazingly large, circular pavement design by **Joan Miró**, which forms the Plaça de Boquería. Remember to look out for the bizarre house at no. 82. Built one hundred years ago as the umbrella store Casa Bruno Quadros, this eccentric design by **Josep Villaseca** is adorned with a large, green dragon over the doorway, under which an open umbrella is rather jauntily hung. Parasols festoon the façade, creating just one of Barcelona's many architectural quirks.

Rambla dels Caputxins **

Pavement cafés and restaurants line the fourth Rambla, which has some interesting diversions in its side streets. The most important feature on the Caputxines, however, is the **Gran Teatre del Liceu** rebuilt in the late 1990s for the fourth time. Facing it, the **Café de l'Opera** is a city landmark, busy day and night – with tourists more than locals but nonetheless atmospheric. Behind the Liceu, west of the Rambla is one of the city's most sleazy areas, the **Barri Xines**. Riddled with criminals, sex shops and porn shows amid general scenes of inner city poverty, this is not a place to stroll alone at night. By day it's less menacing and does have some excellent, very authentic tapas and absinthe (gin) bars as well as a couple of important sights.

Plaça del Pi ***

Signposted from the Rambla, Plaça del Pi is a beautiful, shady square with a weekend market selling local produce including beeswax candles, mountain honey, goats cheese and jars of quince jelly. The square is named after the pine tree at its centre, and orange trees, heavy with fruit in spring, provide some shade in which to enjoy a *café con leche*. The whole square is dominated by the huge bulk of the church of **Santa María del Pi** and is always busy with buskers because of the excellent acoustics provided by the old houses and the solid stone of the church.

LICEU

Barcelona's Liceu, once one of Europe's largest opera houses with a capacity of over 5000, has a history riddled with disaster. The pride of the city, the building was founded in 1847. Destroyed by fire in 1861, it was rebuilt and soon became the talk of Europe, attracting legendary figures of Italian and German opera. In 1893, two bombs were thrown onto the stage during a performance of William Tell, killing 20 people. The theatre was repaired again. Then in January 1994, a worker's blowtorch set fire to some scenery, razing the building to the ground. Yet again, the opera house rose from the ashes.

Left: *Beautiful old façades adorn the sunlit buildings around the Plaça del Pi.*

Below: *The elegant
Plaça Reial is a popular
meeting place.*

There are several fascinating buildings around the
square. The **Casa Josep Roca**, with its warm coffee-and-
beige façade, is the city's oldest hardware store, with
gleaming cutlery displays still gracing its window. The
farmácia, too, with its elaborate black and gold window,
is typical of turn-of-the-century *modernista* design. In
another corner, a doorway leads to Les Galeries Maldà, a
fancy modern arcade specializing in jewellery shops.

Església de Santa María del Pi ★
Built in the 14th century, burned badly in the civil war of
1936 and carefully restored in the 1960s, the church is
Gothic in style. Rather austere on the outside, the interior
is stunning, a vast rose window throwing multicoloured
sunbeams across the cool flagstones.

On the other side of the church is another charming
square, **Plaça de Sant Josep Oriol**. At weekends there's
an excellent art market here, local painters displaying
their surprisingly good wares.

Plaça Reial ★★
Quite a contrast to the shady Plaça del Pi, the Plaça Reial,
through an archway a little further along the Rambla, is a
large, wide open square bordered by tall, elegant buildings, all painted in the same shade of imperial yellow.

Left: *Stamp collectors compare notes at the Sunday market on the Plaça Reial.*

Palm trees are dotted around the square, which was built in the 19th century on the site of a convent, and a fountain in the middle depicts the Three Graces. Around the base of the buildings, arches and porticoes bear motifs of the exploration of the New World. Nowadays, these archways are home to a string of bars and cafés and the square has a bustling atmosphere. At weekends there's a thriving coin and stamp market, dealers coming from miles around to display their wares on long trestle tables. Look out for the ornate lampposts dotted around the square – they are originals by the young Gaudí.

Rambla de Santa Monica *

In its final stretch, the Rambla widens out onto the seafront. A craft market is usually in evidence here, selling touristy souvenirs and cheap costume jewellery. There are a couple of points of interest; the 17th-century **Convent of Santa Monica** now holds temporary art exhibitions and the **Palau March** opposite, a neoclassical building from the late 18th century, houses the Department de Cultura de la Generalitat. At the bottom of the street, on the left, is Barcelona's **Museu de Cera**, or wax museum, which houses a collection of wax figures from the world of politics and entertainment. Open 10:00–14:00 and 16:00–20:00 Monday–Friday, 10:00–20:00 Saturday–Sunday. From here, the Rambla opens out into the port, the view dominated by a towering monument to Columbus.

BARRI XINES

The Barri Xines is not a particularly inspiring part of Barcelona but does have its claim to fame. Serious Picasso fans should take a stroll along the **carrer d'Avinyo**, the stately houses of which were converted to brothels at the turn of the century. The young Picasso used to spend hours sketching scenes from the street and claims to have had his first sexual experience in one of the brothels. The women from these brothels are said to have inspired the famous *Les Demoiselles d'Avignon* in 1907.

Barri Xines

There are, in fact, no Chinese people living in the 'Chinatown' district of Barcelona, the area to the right of the Rambla, walking towards the sea. The district gets its name simply because its clubs and sex shops reminded visitors between the wars of similar red light districts in their own towns. The area's proper name is **El Raval** and it extends from the west side of the Rambla to the port, bordered in the north by the carrer de Hospital, with several worthwhile sights in its narrow streets.

Palau Güell **

On the right hand side of the Rambla at Nou de la Rambla 3 is one of Antoni Gaudí's early *modernista* works, the Palau Güell. Built in 1885 for Don Eusebio Güell, a wealthy shipowner, the Palace now houses the Theatre Museum. Notable features include the vast, heavy balcony over the entrance with its intricate iron work and the bizarre, twisted chimney stacks covered with colourful tiles, a Gaudí trademark. Inside, the influence of Gaudí is visible in the undulating columns and archways. Open 10:00–13:00, 17:00–19:00 Monday–Friday. Closed on weekends.

EUSEBIO GUELL

The wealthy shipowner and industrialist Eusebio Güell (1846–1918) was the main patron of Gaudí from 1878, when they met, until 1918 when Güell died aged 71. Güell commissioned some of Gaudí's most important works, including the Palau Güell just off the Rambla, the Parc Güell, intended by the patron to be an exclusive housing estate but in the end inhabited only by himself and Gaudí. Güell was such an admirer of Gaudí's work that he arranged a special exhibition of the architect's achievement in Paris in 1910. The exhibition was a success although Gaudí failed to attend, sinking instead into a deep depression.

Sant Pau de Camp *

Along the Carrer Sant Pau, in the heart of the Barri Xines, is this magnificent Catalan Romanesque church. It is the city's oldest church. Perhaps the most sensible time to visit this church would be between 18:00–19:00, before evening mass. The name *Camp* means 'plains'; when it was built in the 10th century, the church would have been some distance from the city walls, surrounded by fields. The church was once a Benedictine abbey and now holds services at 08:00 on weekdays and four times on Sunday. The naive carvings above the door date back to the 13th century.

Hospital de la Santa Creu *

On carrer de Hospital in the northern part of the Barri Xines, a cluster of Gothic buildings form the Hospital de la Santa Creu. It was built in 1410 to modernize and bring together the services of several other hospitals. The main building now houses the National Library. In the **Casa de Convalescència**, look for the ceramic tiles in the courtyard.

Museu d'Art Contemporani de Barcelona **

This futuristic museum is quite a contrast to its setting on the busy Plaça dels Angels on the edge of the Barri Xines. Stark white walls, glossy black floors, glass and granite offset over 1000 works by Calder, Miró and Klee (among others), with sunlight filtering through the opalescent blinds. Richard Meier, the building's American architect, describes it as 'a cathedral of our time'. The building is set on three levels with sweeping views over the clustered rooftops of the old city from the top floor. In a way it symbolizes or reflects the vital role which the city has played in the history of modern art. Open June–September 11:00–20:00 Monday, Wednesday, Friday; 11:00–21:00 Thursday; 10:00–20:00 Saturday and 10:00–15:00 Sunday. October–May 11:00–19:30 Monday, Wednesday, Friday; 11:00–20:00 Saturday and 10:00–15:00 Sunday.

Left: *The stunning Museum of Contemporary Art, a temple to modernity.*
Opposite: *The lavish interior of the Palau Güell.*

THE SEAFRONT

Barcelona's run down seafront was completely transformed for the 1992 Olympic Games. The crumbling old docks were turned into glamorous yacht marinas and a new promenade, **Moll de la Fusta**, once a timber wharf, now connects the Columbus statue to the eastern corner of the Barri Gòtic. In summer, this is packed with people strolling in the sun, admiring the yachts. From just below the Columbus monument, small passenger boats, **Las Golondrinas**, leave on half-hourly sightseeing tours of the harbour. The strange metal towers are not part of the docks; they are stations for the panoramic cable car which makes the thrilling descent from **Montjuïc** and across the harbour to **Barceloneta**. The cable car runs from 12:00–19:00 daily in fine weather.

Columbus Monument *

A city landmark, this 50m (164ft) tower was designed by Gaietà Buiges in 1886 for the 1888 Expo, with Columbus perched on top, pointing out to sea. The explorer was received in Barcelona in 1493 by the Catholic King and Queen, Ferdinand and Isabella, on his return from his first voyage to the New World. A cramped lift inside whisks passengers to the top of the tower with sweeping views across the city and docks, although scratched Perspex windows make it almost impossible to photograph the scene. Open 10:00–13:30, 15:30–18:30 Monday–Saturday, 10:00–18:30 Sunday.

SPANISH POLICE

There are three types of police in Spain. In rural locations, the most prolific are the Guardia Civil, founded in 1848 by the Duque de Amuhada to fight bandits in the countryside. Guardia Civil wear green uniforms with black tricorn hats and handle traffic offences and law and order generally. Smaller towns have a Policía Municipal, who wear navy blue and deal with local crimes and urban traffic control. They are funded by the town hall. Towns with a population of more than 20,000 also have a Policía Nacional force, funded by the government and armed with machine guns. Policía Nacional, who wear navy blue, are responsible for dealing with serious crime on a nationwide basis.

Maremagnum *

Surrounded by such spectacular architecture, it seems ironic that the residents of Barcelona should be so taken with a modern shopping mall. Nonetheless, whole families flock to the glassy Maremagnum Centre at weekends to feast on tapas and American ice cream, visit the multiplex cinemas and browse the expensive designer shops.

The approach to Maremagnum is impressive, over acres of dark wooden decking and a futuristic wooden drawbridge which opens to allow yachts to exit the harbour. In winter, people crowd the wooden benches, warmed by the weak sun, and watch athletes rowing in the harbour.

For a wet day, there's plenty to pass the time at Maremagnum. As well as the shops and the multi-screen cinema, there's an **aquarium** with an underwater walk through a Perspex tunnel, sharks circling overhead. At the **Imax** theatre, you can experience the cinema of the future. On a giant screen, the height of a five-storey apartment block, crystal-clear images and surround-sound whisk the viewer across the dusty plains of the Serengeti or plunging over the edge of the Grand Canyon.

Museu Maritim **

Just behind the Columbus statue the **Reials Drassanes**, Barcelona's 13th-century Royal shipyards, have been put to fitting use as the home of the Maritime Museum. Today, the high, stone-vaulted ceilings protect a spectacular copy of a 16th-century royal barge as well as countless smaller vessels. Maps, compasses and special effects of storms and battles all add to the atmosphere. A raised catwalk allows one to admire the interior roof structure and to see the exhibits from a different angle from above. Open Monday–Friday 10:00–13:30 and 16:00–19:30, Saturday, Sunday and holidays 10:00–13:30 and 16:30–20:00.

> **WORKING IN CATALUNYA**
>
> With unemployment fairly high in Catalunya, the chances of finding a stimulating job are thin. There is, however, casual work to be found for the summer season in the coastal resorts, where bartending and waitressing jobs come up every spring. Wages are low but there are plenty of takers keen to spend a summer in the sun. Jobs can also be found in the marinas along the coast, scrubbing decks and occasionally, as crew on large yachts.

Below: *The Museu Maritim is packed with historical artefacts, many of them from wrecked ships.*
Opposite: *Barcelona's waterfront has found new life since redevelopment in 1992.*

3
Barri Gòtic

Barcelona's Gothic quarter seems to have changed little since the 15th century, when the maze of streets was encircled by protective walls. Here, you'll find dark, narrow alleys, shafts of sunlight filtering down through the tall buildings and iron balconies draped with greenery. Overhead, washing flaps from every window and at ground level there are tiny, brightly lit tapas bars where the Barri's residents, many of them elderly, gather after the nightly *passeig*.

Every so often, the tangle of streets opens out onto a cobbled square, flanked by beautiful, medieval Gothic palaces and, of course, the brooding bulk of Barcelona's magnificent cathedral, **La Seu**. Linger for a while at dusk when the setting sun has turned the tops of the buildings pink and the only sound is a lone busker's haunting flute melody echoing from the cathedral steps.

There's plenty to see in the Barri Gòtic and the best way to appreciate it is on foot. As well as the cathedral and crumbling **Roman walls**, there are the ornate **Generalitat** and **Ajuntament** buildings, the **Museu Mares** and the **Palau Episcopal**. The **Museu d'Història de la Ciutat**, meanwhile, provides a fascinating insight into the city's past.

By night, this area is fairly lively, particularly in summer and there are some excellent, very old restaurants to explore as well as some genuinely local bars. Picasso fans should not miss the opportunity of a drink in **Els Quatre Gats**, the café once frequented by the artist and his contemporaries.

DON'T MISS

*** La Seu: Barcelona's magnificent cathedral.
*** Museu d'Història de la Ciutat: the city's history under one roof.
** Plaça Reial: beautiful square surrounded by medieval palaces.
* Els Quatre Gats: have a drink in Picasso's old haunt.

Opposite: *The impressive exterior of Catedral de Santa Eulàlia, better known as La Seu.*

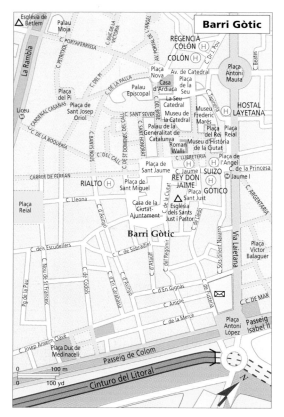

PLAÇA DE SANT JAUME

At the heart of the Barri Gòtic, the cobbled Plaça de Sant Jaume has witnessed all aspects of city life over the centuries, from the bustle of a Roman street market to modern day political demonstrations.

On the west side, the 15th-century **Palau de la Generalitat de Catalunya** has been home to the government since 1977. Unfortunately, the building is only open on St George's Day. Long queues form to get inside and admire the Gothic arcades surrounding the inner courtyard and the gold coffered ceiling of the **Saló Daurat**, a medieval conference hall. The **Chapel of St Jordi** dates back to the 15th century although the façade of the building is more recent, from the late 16th century.

Ajuntament *

Opposite the Generalitat is the town hall, **Casa de la Ciutat** in Catalan, a stern-looking structure with a 19th-century, neoclassical façade. In April 1931, the Spanish Republic was proclaimed from the balcony of this building. Older parts of the building date back to the 14th century and the Saló de Cent, the meeting room of the former 'Council of 100' (*see* p. 10) has a magnificent, 15th-century floor in red and yellow, the national colours of Catalunya. Inside there are statues, wonderfully decorated halls and a sweeping staircase.

Jewish Quarter *
Around the Gothic quarter is the Call, Barcelona's former Jewish quarter, stretching from Banys Nous to carrer de la Palla. Little remains of the city's once thriving Jewish community although on carrer Marlet at no. 1 is the poignant sight of a small plaque bearing Hebrew inscriptions. Today, the narrow streets of the Call are lined with cheap costume jewellery wholesalers, whose wares reappear every day in the tourist stalls on the Rambla.

Sants Justs i Pastor *
Located behind the Ajuntament, this is supposedly Barcelona's oldest church, although most of the building is 14th-century. It was once the parish church for the Count-Kings of Barcelona and Aragón, and the place where early Christians worshipped. Today the beautiful stained glass and intricate stone inside make the church very popular for weddings.

Temple of Augustus *
From the Plaça de Sant Jaume towards the Plaça del Rei is a spectacular relic of Roman Barcelona, a temple dating back to AD100. All that remains today are four columns around a small courtyard.

JEWISH BARCELONA

A Jewish ghetto thrived for 300 years in the dark alleys of the Gothic quarter until the Spanish Jews were persecuted during the inquisition. As early as the 13th century there were stirrings of anti-Semitism and Jews had to wear special distinguishing clothes. Furthermore, the Jewish community was falsely held responsible by the Catholic kings for the plague in Barcelona and finally expelled in 1424, after which time the synagogues were destroyed or converted into churches.

Below: *Dragons are the central theme of St George's Day, 23 April.*

Right: *Imposing buildings with high stone arches surround the Plaça del Rei.*

PLAÇA DEL REI

This magical square is virtually unchanged since medieval times, a hidden corner of the Gothic quarter surrounded by awe-inspiring palaces, stone doorways allowing the occasional glimpse into a shady courtyard. Once the home of the Counts of Barcelona, the square today is a peaceful place with excellent acoustics. Recitals are often held here and there are always buskers by day. On the sweeping steps of the **Saló de Tinell**, Ferdinand and Isabella received Columbus on his return from the discovery of the New World. A more sinister memory held in the building's dense stone walls is the echo of meetings that were held here during the Spanish Inquisition. Open 10:00–20:00 Monday–Saturday, 10:00–16:00 Sunday.

On one corner of the square is a five storey medieval watchtower and the **Capella de Santa Agata**, a pretty 14th-century chapel with exquisite stained glass windows.

Museu d'Història de la Ciutat ★★

The other building on the square, **Palau Clariana Padellas**, housing the Museu d'Història de la Ciutat, has an unusual history. Originally located on the carrer de

Mercaders, the Palace was in the way of a proposed new road and in 1931 was moved to the Plaça del Rei, where it was rebuilt over ancient remains. Other exhibits include a 14th-century Christian basilica and parts of the city's 11th-century Romanesque cathedral, giving the visitor quite a clear idea of the city in former times. Open 10:00–14:00, 16:00–20:00 Tuesday–Saturday, 10:00–14:00 Sunday, 10:00–20:00 July, August and September.

Palau de Lloctinent *

Just off the Plaça del Rei is another lovely old palace, the 16th-century Palace of the Lieutenant. What is believed to be the largest medieval archive in the world – relating to the dynasty of Aragón dating back to the 9th century – is housed here. Sadly, this is not on view to the public, but you can get a glimpse of the tranquil inner courtyard, with splashing fountains and ancient, twisted vines climbing the stone walls.

Museu Frederic Marés **

This eclectic collection is on the carrer dels Comtes in a wing of the Palau Reial Major and was donated to the city by the sculptor Frederic Marés (1893–1991) in 1946. The museum houses most of his collection, consisting largely of sculptures dating from pre-Roman times to the 19th century, including three entire floors of crucifixes. The other part of the museum, the Collector's Room gives a fascinating insight into everyday life in Barcelona from the 15th century to the present, featuring everything from matchboxes to walking sticks. Open 10:00–17:00 Tuesday–Saturday, 10:00–14:00 Sunday.

Below: *Sunlight streams through the graceful arches in the cloisters of La Seu.*

LA SEU AND SURROUNDS

La Seu is in the heart of the Barri Gòtic, facing the Plaça de la Seu. Wherever you walk in the Gothic quarter, the dark mass of the cathedral looms, crammed in between the labyrinth of alleys and the jumble of palaces. The site on which La Seu lies was first a Roman temple and briefly, in Moorish times, a mosque. Open 07:00–13:30 and 16:00–19:30 daily.

Inside, the cathedral used to be dark and rather gloomy because the stained glass windows are placed so high in the walls. Clever lighting, however, has given the building a breathtaking sensation of space, its 25m (80ft) vaulted ceiling soaring high above the gilded chapels below. The cathedral is dedicated to Santa Eulàlia, the female patron saint of Barcelona. Her death and martyrdom in AD304 are illustrated on the 16th-century marble choir screen in the nave, by Ordóñez i Villar. A crypt below the altar contains her tomb.

Around the edge of the cathedral are 29 chapels illuminated by candles. Some of the tombs are impressive, particularly that of Ramón Berenguer I, Count of Barcelona until 1025 and founder of the second Romanesque cathedral on this site.

The cloister is quite a surprise as you emerge blinking into the sunlight. Tall palms and shady magnolias create a tropical garden in the most unlikely setting, completed by a gaggle of vociferous white geese, apparently there to ward off thieves and guard the tomb of Sant Eulàlia.

Just off the cloister is the small **Museu de la Catedral** containing Bartolomé Bermejo's stunning work *La Pietat* (The Devotion) and a 15th-century altarpiece by Catalan painter Huguet (1414–92). Open 11:00–13:00 daily.

Below: *The cathedral's interior is awe-inspiring with its tall, slender columns.*

Left: *Picasso designed this mural on the exterior of the Col.legi d'Arquitectes.*

PLAÇA NOVA

Once on the modern Plaça Nova, facing the main façade of La Seu, the magical atmosphere of the Barri Gòtic ends. Turn around, however, and admire the large chunk of the city's original Roman walls and two more palatial Gothic buildings, the Casa de l'Ardiaca which houses the city archives and the Palau Episcopal, the Bishop's Palace, with the characteristic, shaded central courtyard and outdoor stone stairway. In sharp contrast, directly opposite the cathedral, the giant frieze around the modern Col.legi d'Arquitectes building was done by Picasso in 1960.

Els Quatre Gats *

One more experience that is not to be missed around the Gothic quarter is the legendary bar, Els Quatre Gats (the four cats) at carrer Montsio 3. A group of *modernista* artists opened the bar in 1897 and Puig i Cadafalch designed the interior as his first commission, resulting in a warm, spacious interior of tiled walls and wooden galleries. The bar quickly became the haunt of the city's artistic community and many ideas, magazines and paintings were born here. Picasso's first public exhibition took place in the bar in 1901. Still buzzing with life, the Quatre Gats is a wonderful place to recover after exploring the Gothic quarter, and all sorts of reminders of the golden age of the *modernista* period adorn the walls, not least a large painting by Ramón Casa, of himself and Pere Romeu riding a tandem bicycle.

4
La Ribera

Today the old city is bisected by the busy **Via Laietana**, constructed in 1859 as part of the plans for the Eixample. The area to the east, La Ribera, is as fascinating as the Barri Gòtic in its own way and with the exception of the **carrer Montcada**, home of the legendary **Picasso Museum**, is far less commercial.

La Ribera is a curious mixture of what would have been medieval tenement buildings, and exquisite palaces, still beautifully preserved. Merchants and nobles lived side by side with sailors in the 14th century and while their palaces are now mostly museums and galleries, the Ribera still has a thriving population in its narrow streets with some very lively bars after dark, particularly in the **Passeig del Born** to the east. East of the district, the **Parc de la Ciutadella** (site of the Museu d'Art Modern and the Zoo) forms a natural border to Barcelona's old town, a shady, restful place with some surprising buildings dotted around it, not least one of the seats of the Parliament of Catalunya and an outrageously over-the-top fountain designed by the young Gaudí.

The park was originally the gardens of a citadel built by Felipe V in 1715. Fishermen's houses were razed to the ground to make way for this stronghold and the community moved to **Barceloneta**. Barceloneta's streets are dark and narrow and many of its excellent fish restaurants have been moved on to more respectable locations, but from the cable car it is still possible to see piles of fishing nets and boats bobbing alongside the quay.

Opposite: *In autumn, the weather is still warm enough to enjoy the sun in Ciutadella Park.*

Picasso lived and studied in Barcelona from the age of 13 to 23, arriving in 1895 at the height of the *modernista* movement. The young artist studied at the Llotya Art School but his real inspiration came from the crowd of painters who hung around at the bar Els Quatre Gats. Picasso designed posters promoting the bar and published illustrations in journals of the time.

Picasso's Blue Period evolved in Barcelona, drawing melancholy images from the city's poorer quarters, and even when he moved to France in 1904 he continued to make trips back to the city to paint.

Picasso drew on popular Catalan folklore in many of his paintings. Look for images like people dancing the *Sardana*, Catalunya's national dance; the traditional beret, or *barretina*; doves; the *porro*, Catalunya's typical long spouted wine carafe; and even the Columbus monument on the Rambla. The murals on the side of the Coleg.gi d'Arquitectes portray Palm Sunday palms, traditional dances and the giant figures, or *gegants*, used in parades.

Palau de la Música Catalana ★★

This concert hall, a *modernista* masterpiece by Domènech i Montaner, is squeezed into a tiny alleyway, carrer Sant Pere Mes Alt. Built in 1908 for the **Orfeó Català** choir, the building is spectacular inside and out. A large sculpture, *La Canco Popular Catalana* by Miguel Blay, located on the southeast corner of the building, portrays singers in a choir while the main entrance is adorned with busts of famous musicians including Beethoven and Bach.

CARRER MONTCADA

Barcelona's most popular tourist attraction, the **Picasso Museum**, is located on what many believe to be the city's most beautiful street, carrer Montcada. Here, lovely old patrician buildings have been spruced up, their shady courtyards filled with greenery and heavy, polished wooden doors. Art galleries line the street and even the souvenir shops are tasteful, selling mainly Picasso memorabilia and posters. At no. 14, the Caixa des Pensións gallery is in a 16th-century palace, while the Galeria Maeght at no. 25 is in the Palau dels Cervelló.

Museu Picasso ★★★

Housed in three stunning medieval palaces, the Picasso Museum is beautifully laid out in a series of rooms representing different phases of the artist's life. The huge variation in style illustrates Picasso's incredible talent and diversity.

The museum owns some 3000 of Picasso's works, of which around 500 are on display. The initial collection was donated by Picasso's friend and one-time secretary Jaime Sabartes in 1963 and added to by the artist himself after Sabartes' death in 1968.

If you can understand the Spanish and Catalan instructions, follow the rooms in chronological order. Picasso's early works consist of whole rooms of tiny sketches and studies and some major portraits painted when he was a teenager in Barcelona. There are several scenes of the city; particularly interesting is a watercolour of Barceloneta in 1897, which was nothing but a tiny, low-rise fishing village in those days.

Below: *The Picasso Museum is housed in a series of medieval palaces.*

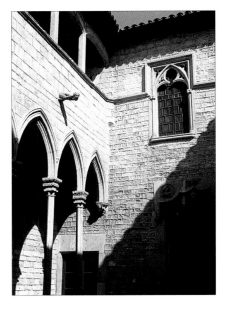

Examples from Picasso's various periods follow, with a fabulous collection from his Blue Period **(1901–04)**, Pink Period **(1904–06)** and later Cubist and neoclassical phases. Some of the most spectacular paintings are from 1957, dazzling blues and acid greens of his time in Cannes, the study of the Velázquez masterpiece, *Las Meninas*, and the scarlet-and-lime of his portraits of his wife Jacqueline, which occupy five rooms. Don't miss the ceramics either, a collection of 41 pieces donated by Jacqueline in 1981.

The museum also has a library for serious researchers and downstairs, a charming café and excellent shop selling prints of virtually everything in the museum and some comprehensive books. Open 10:00–20:00 Tuesday–Saturday, 10:00–15:00 Sunday.

MUSEUMS

On the first Sunday of the month, entrance to Barcelona's municipal museums, which includes the **Museu Picasso**, the **Museu d'Història de la Ciutat**, the **Textile Museum** and the **Pedralbes monastery** is free. Separate exhibitions within the museums still incur a charge. Almost all museums are closed on a Monday, so plan your itinerary carefully. An excellent guide, *Barcelona Museums*, which gives full details of things like disabled access, is available free from the tourist board.

Below: *Magnificent stained glass windows adorn the Santa María del Mar.*

Museu Tèxtil i d'Indumentària ★★

Like many other galleries and museums in this street, the textile museum is housed in an old palace, once belonging to the Marques de Llió. Typical of Gothic noblemen's houses, the building has a central courtyard and an outside stone staircase. In the elegant halls around this central feature is a vast collection of fabrics from the 4th to the 20th centuries including lace, tapestry, clothing and accessories ranging from fans to hair ornaments. There is also an exhibition of tools from the Catalan textile industry and a showroom of outfits from the great couturiers including Balenciaga and Pedro Rodríguez. Open 10:00–17:00 Tuesday–Saturday, 10:00–14:00 Sunday.

Santa María del Mar ★★

At the bottom of the carrer Montcada is another of Barcelona's great Gothic churches, Santa María del Mar, dedicated to the patron saint of sailors. Built in 1323 by architect Berenguer de Montagut on what was then the seafront, the fortress-like church is considered to be one of the finest examples of Gothic Catalan architecture because of the purity of its lines.

The interior is touchingly simple: one vast, beautiful rose window and further pieces of jewel-like stained glass are virtually the only treasures which did not disappear in the civil war. A carved wooden sailing ship rests on the simple Baroque altar.

Passeig del Born

The scruffy but atmospheric Passeig del Born, running from the church up to the old marketplace, **Antic Mercat del Born**, was a hive of activity during the Middle Ages. Jousting competitions and fairs took place here and much later, in the 19th century, the market was one of the city's largest. Now it's

an exhibition hall. The *passeig* itself is lined with stone benches on which old people gossip and read the paper or drink in the many tapas bars. These are not the sleek designer bars of the Passeig de Gràcia, however; more like plastic and formica, with the television blaring a football match commentary in a corner.

LA LLOTJA

Heading in the opposite direction from the church towards the sea, the graceful Llotja, once home to the **Consolat de Mar**, which regulated sea traffic and later the trading exchange, stands out on Plaça Antoní Lopez. Now the home of Barcelona's stock exchange, the building contains wide arches around a central courtyard, typical of Catalan Gothic architecture. The exterior, however, is more recent, renovated in the late 18th century. Graceful, white marble statues adorn the neoclassical façade and roof.

Opposite, on the Passeig Isabel II are the **Porxos d'en Xifré**, an elegant arcade built in 1836 by Josep Xifré, who had made his fortune in the American colonies. The buildings today house various electronics shops and one of Barcelona's most famous restaurants, the very grand **Set Portes**.

Above: *Typical of Catalan Gothic architecture, La Llotja houses the city's stock exchange.*

LOS CARACOLES

Los Caracoles, a rambling establishment in the carrer Escudellers, deep in the Barri Gòtic, claims to be Barcelona's oldest restaurant. Decorated like an old Catalan house with giant hams and bunches of herbs and garlic hanging from the low, beamed ceilings, the restaurant is always buzzing. Europe's glitterati were certainly attracted to Los Caracoles in the 1940s and 1950s, and signed black-and-white celebrity photos adorn every wall. For such a big tourist attraction, the food is very good and typically Catalan, including snails in garlic, spit-roast chicken, giant fragrant paella and the best *crema catalana* in town.

Above: *The former fisherman's quarter of Barceloneta now overlooks gleaming yachts, not fishing smacks.*

VIEWS OF BARCELONA

You can arrive at Barceloneta in style by cable car, a breath-taking descent from Montjuïc on a wire supported by only two towers spanning the entire waterfront. This is also a good way to see the old fishing port, with nets piled up on the wharf. Other sweeping views of the city are to be had from the top of Tibidabo; the dizzying spires of the Sagrada Família (only for the brave; the lift emerges onto a narrow stone bridge between two spires); the wave bench in the Parc Güell and, if you're lucky enough to stay there, the upper floors of the deluxe Hotel Arts, the futuristic tower overlooking Barceloneta.

BARCELONETA

This wedge-shaped grid pattern of housing jutting out into the harbour was built /in 1755 on what used to be sand flats. As Felipe V proceeded with the construction of his citadel, 52 streets and 1200 houses were destroyed and their inhabitants, mainly fishermen, were rehoused in the new development, 'Little Barcelona'. The new houses were built on long, straight, narrow streets punctuated by small squares and each building was only two storeys high with unusually large windows, the idea being to let in as much light as possible. These became largely redundant, however, as more floors were added and the streets of Barceloneta ended up being rather dark.

To this day, Barceloneta is famous for its fish restaurants, known for serving the freshest fish at the best prices, which line the main streets on either side of the wedge. In the pre-Olympic clean up, however, most of the semi-illegal beach restaurants (where diners would sit with their feet in the sand) were closed down and only those on the pleasant, tree-lined **Passeig de Borbó** which faces the harbour remain.

Many of the other beach restaurants have been shifted to the port's one time general warehouse, the **Palau de Mar**, overlooking the marina. In the evenings, after a *passeig* along Moll de la Fusta, this is a great, if expensive place to enjoy the balmy air and watch the last streaks of pink in the sky fade over Montjuïc.

Parc de Mar and the Vila Olímpica *

Anyone who knew Barcelona before the Olympic Games agrees that the glossy new seafront development of the Vila Olímpica is nothing short of a miracle. Dreary, run-down docks have been converted into a 5km (3 mile) stretch of futuristic offices, modern housing and landscaped parks. The whole complex is connected to the airport by a new highway that goes along the seafront and cuts round the foot of **Montjuïc**.

Two steel-and-glass towers dominate the shoreline, one a hotel and the other an office block, a gleaming new marina lined with bars and restaurants at their base. Opposite is the Olympic Village, designed to host the 15,000 athletes and the Games, although the story goes that many of the competitors, unable to tolerate the punishing summer heat, took refuge in the air-conditioned, five star Hotel Arts, the tower with the steel-framed exterior. The brilliantly coloured sculpture opposite Barceloneta was designed by Roy Lichtenstein and is called **Barcelona Head**.

Opponents of the development, who would rather have seen lower cost housing than the smart apartments of the Vila Olímpica, are smug in the knowledge that the property did not sell quickly. But residents of the new houses seem happy enough with the local infrastructure, and during the summer months the bars around the marina are packed with locals eating, drinking and strolling. Young people in particular are attracted to the lively, fashionable bars with views over the marina, and in summer, the area is buzzing until the small hours. The area should have a further injection of life with the planned opening of cinema and shopping complexes.

Below: *Roy Lichtenstein's colourful* 'Barcelona Head' *sculpture exemplifies the contemporary feel of Barcelona.*

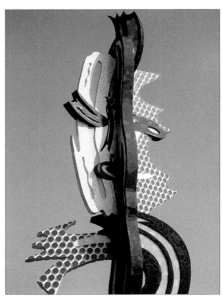

OPEN AIR BARCELONA

Don't miss the *Grec* season in July and August, a summer festival of outdoor entertainment centred around the open air Greek theatre on Montjuïc. June also sees the Dìa de Sant Joan festival on the 23rd when fireworks are set off all over the city, and the Caixa flamenco festival in the same month, when the town's Andalucían population parties late into the night.

Below: *The extravagant Cascade fountain was one of Gaudí's early efforts in design.*

PARC DE LA CIUTADELLA

Central Barcelona is strangely lacking in green spaces. Areas of the Eixample which were allocated for parkland were quickly developed as the city grew. New green areas were created in 1992 for the Olympics but prior to that, Montjuïc, the Parc Güell and the Parc de la Ciutadella were the only areas where people could jog and walk their dogs. This particular park is named after the fortified citadel built by Felipe V in 1715 to keep the city under control after it resisted his cause in the War of Spanish Succession. Much of the citadel was destroyed in 1869 to make way for a park and what remains of the Baroque palace is today the seat of the Catalan parliament and the **Museum of Modern Art**.

Scattered around the park is also an eclectic collection of buildings designed for the 1888 Universal Exposition. To the north is a vast **Arc de Triomf**, a mock-Mudéjar arch by Josep Vilaseca serving as the entrance to the Expo. The best feature, however, is the outrageous Cascada fountain, designed by architect Josep Fontserè with assistance from the young Gaudí. Now overgrown with moss and creepers, this mock-Baroque extravaganza is topped with winged lions and dramatic horse-drawn chariots, fiery dragons jutting out below.

In contrast, the remainder of the park is an oasis of orange, magnolia and oleander trees, locals walking dogs and people resting under horse chestnuts.

Globo Turistico **

Between Francia station and the zoo is the world's highest tethered balloon. Rise up to a height of 150m (492ft) for stunning views of the city.

Museu de Zoologia *

Just outside the gates is a very grand, red-brick, castle-like building designed by Domènech i Montaner in 1888 as the café for the Expo. Nicknamed the

Castell dels Tres Dragons, the building was used as a centre for arts and crafts and now houses the Zoological Museum which has a collection of stuffed animals as well as a section devoted to living insects. Open 10:00–14:00, Tuesday–Saturday; 10:00–18:00 Thursday.

Above: Parc de la Ciutadella provides vital green space for the city's residents.

Museu de Geologia *

Behind the Zoological Museum is a glass palm house and conservatory, or **Hivernacle**, now a cultural centre, as well as the **Museu Martorell**, the city's first public museum which opened in 1882. Now used as the Geological Museum, the rooms contain a collection of rocks, fossils and minerals. In a corner of the park, Barcelona's **zoo** contains an unusual collection of caged animals, including what is believed to be the world's only captive albino gorilla. Open 10:00–14:00, Tuesday–Saturday.

Museu d'Art Modern de Catalunya *

With Picasso, Miró, Tàpies and Dalí all in their own, dedicated museums, there's nothing world-famous in this well laid out collection. The museum nonetheless gives a good insight into mainly Catalan art of the 19th and early 20th centuries, with *modernista* works by Casas (who was a regular at the famous Quatre Gats), Musignol, Mur and Nonell. Sculptures by Gargallo are also featured. Open 10:00–19:00, Tuesday–Saturday; 10:00–14:30 Sunday .

5
Eixample and Gràcia

Towards the end of the 19th century it became clear that Gothic Barcelona was going to have to expand. By now, the wealth generated by Spain's American colonies and the first Industrial Revolution was giving rise to a national rebirth of art and literature – a latter-day renaissance. A modern extension to Barcelona was planned, the Ensanche (in Castilian Spanish) or **Eixample** (in Catalan), as it is known today.

In 1854, the old city walls were demolished and from 1860, plans drawn up by the city planner Ildefons Cerdà were implemented, creating a vast grid system of streets perpendicular and parallel to the sea. The plan dictated that residential blocks would have green inner court-yards and shaved corners, creating an impression of space and light. The proportion of open space to build-ings was to be 2:1. Three broad boulevards, **Diagonal**, **Gran Via** and **Meridiana** would converge at the **Plaça de les Glòries**, the geographical heart of the new city.

While the Eixample was built according to plan, human nature was quick to rebel against Cerdà's dream of a new, green city. Parks were built over and the court-yards were filled in with more buildings. Plaça de les Glòries never became the heart of the city either, the bourgeoisie choosing to leave and live on the fashionable **Passeig de Gràcia**, where they commissioned young architects to design adventurous houses that were soon to become city status symbols. The working classes, mean-while, remained to the east of the city and factories were built close to the sea alongside Spain's first railway line.

DON'T MISS

*** Sagrada Família: Gaudí's famous cathedral, an unfinished masterpiece.
*** La Pedrera: one of the best examples of *modernista* architecture.
*** Casa Batlló: the most bizarre of the *modernista* buildings, designed around the theme of a dragon.
** Passeig de Gràcia: for stylish shopping.
* Eixample: packed with designer tapas bars.

Opposite: *Gaudí's La Pedrera is now a sought-after apartment block.*

PASSEIG DE GRÀCIA

Barcelona's most fashionable street, the Passeig de Gràcia is 60m (197ft) wide and 1km (⅝mile) long, lined with designer shops, banks, insurance companies and expensive city apartments. But less than 200 years ago, Passeig de Gràcia was a dusty country lane, linking the walled Barcelona to the village of Gràcia. Five lanes were constructed in 1827 and by 1861, the Passeig had regular coach traffic. There was even a horse-drawn tram in the street's heyday, before the advent of the motor car.

What did come out of the Eixample, though, was an exciting new expression in architecture, *modernista*, giving young artists a chance to experiment freely with new construction techniques using iron and cement adorned with tiles and mosaics. The results were extraordinary; fantastic, undulating buildings where animal features sit next to miniature castles, and at the centre the biggest fantasy of all, Gaudí's magnificent church, the **Temple de la Sagrada Família**.

Below: *The city's busiest shopping street, the Passeig de Gràcia.*

The Eixample and **Gràcia** were, and still are, extremely popular places to live and work. The Passeig de Gràcia is the city's most stylish street and the location of several fashionable bars and restaurants, while Gràcia itself, once a hamlet north of the walled city, has never lost its special village atmosphere.

ARCHITECTURAL WALKING TOUR

By far the best way to admire the architecture of the Eixample is on foot, a pleasant ramble through the elegant streets with occasional diversions into coffee shops and museums, starting and finishing at the Passeig de Gràcia metro. Where possible, try to look

inside each building. They are mostly privately owned but the hallways, particularly in Casa Batlló and La Pedrera are as extraordinary as the exteriors.

Above: *The Passeig de Gràcia was originally a horse and carriage track to the village of Gràcia.*

Mansana de la Discòrdia ★★★

Immediately south of the metro station on the right is the famous **Block of Discord**, a trio of extraordinary buildings including one of Gaudí's most famous. The name speaks for itself; a result of the striking differences in style between the Casa Lleó Morera, the Casa Ametller and the Casa Batlló. While the buildings are not open to the public, you can get into the lobby to admire the interiors.

Casa Lleó Morera ★

The first house, Casa Lleó Morera at no. 35, was built by Domènech i Montaner (1850–1923) in 1905. Probably the least ornate of the three, the house is nonetheless distinctive for its huge, semicircular balconies and colourful entrance of inlaid wood and intricate mosaics of fruits and flowers. It is not open to the public.

Perfume Museum ★

Next door is the tiny perfume museum. Hundreds of bottles line the museum's shelves ranging from miniatures of pearl-frosted ampoules from Roman times to ornate Chinese pots. Designs from all the great perfume houses through the ages form a more current display. Open 10:30–13:00, 17:00–19:30 daily. Entrance is free.

CASA FUSTER

With more time to walk around the Eixample, head further north along the Passeig de Gràcia (across Diagonal) to Casa Fuster no. 132, a later work by Domènech i Montaner, built in 1908. The architect's style had matured by the time he designed this building and it carries typical Domènech traits of columns, engraved floral features and dramatic towers, in this case cleverly designed to fit onto a corner block.

Casa Ametller ★

This house, at Passeig de Gràcia 41, was built by Josep Puig i Cadafalch for a Catalan chocolate manufacturer in 1898. The architect experimented with a variety of styles: a Flemish, stepped gable, apricot-and-cream frescoes on the façade, wrought iron balconies and Mudéjar-inspired tiling in the lobby. Inside are wood-beamed ceilings and a vast atrium, light filtering in coloured pools through the Art Nouveau stained glass ceiling. A wonderful, old, wooden cage lift creaks up and down. The detail even on the lights is amazing, hissing dragons rear out from shiny brass fittings under stained glass shades, representing the Catalan theme of St George and the Dragon.

Many of the furnishings are by the same architect and can be seen by paying a visit to the **Institut Ametller d'Art Hispanic** on the first floor. Open 10:00–13:30, Monday–Friday, 15:30–19:00, Tuesday–Thursday.

Casa Batlló ★★★

The interpretation of St George and the Dragon is some-what more dramatic in Gaudí's fabulous Casa Batlló at no. 43, where he added a new façade to an existing building owned by the industrialist, Josep Batlló. The whole building has dragon-like qualities; turquoise, brown and green mosaics make up the façade and the roof undulates like a scaly dragon's back. Concrete almost appears to drip from the overhanging ledges like folds of skin. Window frames resemble bleached bones, presumably of the dragon's victims, while the iron balconies stare like malevolent eyes or animal skulls. On the roof, the cross-shaped chimney represents the sword of St George piercing the dragon's back.

This bizarre design continues in the lobby with a lizard skin motif, painstakingly painted on to the atrium walls. The concierge sits in a kind of cave and staircases disappear in stone

Below: *Casa Ametller was originally built for a chocolate manufacturer.*

Left: *Twisted wire on the roof of Fundació Tàpies gives an idea of the style inside.*

tunnels down into the basement. Even the tiny windows have a scaly pattern. The building is privately owned and although it can be rented out for corporate cocktail parties, passers-by will not get further than the lobby.

Casa Montaner i Simon *

Left into the carrer d'Aragó is the Casa Montaner i Simon, impossible to miss as it's the only building in the street with a giant tangle of wire on the roof, a tribute to the artist whose work is housed inside.

One of the earliest *modernista* works, built in 1880 by Domènech i Montaner, the building was originally the headquarters of a publishing company. Now it is home to the **Fundació Tàpies**, where its industrial feel, high ceilings and spacious halls make the ideal setting for the avant-garde, abstract work of Antoni Tàpies.

Tàpies himself set up the foundation here in 1984. While the main space is given over to international contemporary art exhibitions, Tàpies' work is displayed in the old printing hall. The twisted wire on the roof gives a good idea of what to expect; plenty of experimentation with textures and materials such as junk, metal, wood, newspaper, string and wire. Symbolic themes run through the work; like his contemporaries, Tàpies was outraged and depressed by the civil war, hence the bullet holes and cracks in the later pieces. Upstairs there's a private library and at the entrance, a small shop. Open 11:00–20:00, Tuesday–Sunday.

ANTONI TÀPIES

Tàpies was born in Barcelona in 1923. In 1945, his early works began to appear in public, experimenting with collages of paper, string and wire. His first important exhibition was in New York in the 1950s, featuring the collages and a series of abstract works. Later pieces include more experimentation with texture and assorted political statements, expressed by bullet holes and strange cracks in his canvases. Tàpies continues to be a figure of controversy. Some see him as a talented story-teller and others dismiss him as having an incoherent line of thought.

East of Passeig de Gràcia ★★

Take a detour right into carrer de Mallorca to see two Domènech i Montaner buildings. **Palau Montaner**, set back from the street in a lush garden patrolled by watchful guards, is a rather austere structure livened up by its coppery roof trim and the ornate mosaics of its façade. Across the road at no. 291 is **Casa Thomas**, peppered with blue and yellow tiles and sporting a different balcony design on each of its five floors. Visitors are allowed inside to see the furniture showroom. Look out for the vast, solid wooden door and the painted, wood-beamed ceiling. The remainder of the building is private apartments. Open 10:00–14:00 and 16:00–19:00, Monday–Friday, 10:00–14:00, Saturday.

Above: *The 'house of spikes' looks like something out of a fairytale.*

Casa de les Punxes ★

Turn left onto carrer del Bruc and left again onto Diagonal and look across the road at the startling **Casa Terrades**, better known as **Casa de les Punxes** for its fairytale appearance; tall, conical spires, colourful tiles and a gabled roof. The house was designed by Puig in 1903.

Palau del Baró de Quadras ★

Another, almost Gothic structure by Puig, the house of the barons of Quadras has an ornate façade and a somewhat bizarre roof resembling a row of Alpine chalets. The city's **Music Museum** is here now, housing a collection of instruments from all over the world. Open 10:00–14:00, Tuesday–Sunday, 17:00–20:00, Wednesday.

Casa Comalat ★

Opposite, at no. 442 is Casa Comalat, which at first glance looks like a primitive Gaudí with its undulating forms, eye-like windows and lavish, shiny green roof. This is, however, the work of **Salvador Valeri** (1873–1954), a disciple of Gaudí. Not open to the public.

WHERE TO DRINK

Different types of drinking establishment have different names in Catalunya, which means you're unlikely to get a glass of wine in a *cerveceria*. These specialize in beer. If you want wine, try a *bodega*. A *cockteleria*, meanwhile, serves spirits, while a *xampanyeria* concentrates on cava, or sparkling wine. The *bars modernos* along the Passeig de Gràcia are best interpreted as designer bars – modern, flashy with a wealthy clientele.

Casa Casas and Vinçon **

Back on the Passeig de Gràcia, on the left hand side is one of Barcelona's best-known style shops, Vinçon. This huge, ultra-modern design emporium holds regular furniture design shows in its gallery, once studio of the artist Ramón Casas. Everything is expensive, but for browsing, the store is a tourist attraction in itself. There are plenty of smaller items for sale as souvenirs. Open 10:00–14:00, 16:30–20:30, Monday–Saturday.

La Pedrera ***

Casa Milà, as it is correctly known, is one of Gaudí's most impressive creations, a huge apartment house that covers a whole block (corner of Passeig de Gràcia and carrer de Provença), its roughly finished stone exterior moulded and rounded to resemble cave dwellings. This rock-like appearance gave the building its name, La Pedrera, which means 'quarry'. The wrought iron balconies form strange, organic shapes and the twisted chimney stacks like human forms. Apartments in the building are highly prized.

Tours are conducted in a variety of languages at 11:00, 12:00, 13:00, 16:00 and 17:00 daily, 10:00, 11:00 and 12:00, Saturday–Sunday. The roof terrace opens as a bar with live music on Saturdays and Sundays on summer evenings.

SHOPPING CARD

A credit card is a good idea if you're exploring the Passeig de Gràcia, where all the best designer shops are located. Anyone visiting the city for professional reasons will also be supplied with a Shopping Visitor Card. This card gives discounts at various shops which carry an identifying sticker in the window, and is valid for the visitor's length of stay. With it comes a list of participating stores.

Below: *Chimney stacks on La Pedrera stand out among the buildings.*

SAGRADA FAMÍLIA
Temple Expiatori
de la Sagrada Família ★★★

A short metro ride from Passeig de Gràcia is the Sagrada Família, probably Barcelona's most famous landmark and Gaudí's best-known artistic work. Although still half-built, the Temple of the Holy Family can only be described as awe-inspiring. Soaring, 100m (328ft) spires are topped with brilliant colours; concrete drips like icicles from a façade moulded to resemble piles of clouds and giant, cartoon-like inscriptions of 'Sanctus Sanctus Sanctus' encircle the spires. Open 09:00–20:00.

Above: *Cranes are inter-spersed with the graceful spires of the unfinished Sagrada Família.*
Opposite: *People, birds and animals form the detail of the Nativity façade.*

**SAGRADA FAMÍLIA
LANDMARKS**

1890 First designs.
1925 Belltower of
St Barnabus completed.
1926 Death of Gaudí.
1936 Church desecrated
in the Civil War.
1940 Crypt restored.
1954 Passion façade
was constructed.
1977 Bell towers on passion
façade completed.
1995 Vaults on side
aisles constructed.

The History of Sagrada Família

Barcelona was expanding as the Eixample grew and the **Associació de Devots de Sant Josep**, a local religious group, wanted a cathedral for the poor of the 'new' city. The association bought the land and commissioned the architect Francesc de Paula Villar i Lozano; the church was begun in 1882. But Villar soon fell out with the city council and was replaced by Gaudí who, becoming increasingly devout, proposed to build a symbol of the city, bringing together all his previous interpretations of nature in architecture. Every detail was planned, right down to images of birds and flowers from the surrounding countryside.

Gaudí lived on the site and worked on his dream until his death in 1926, by which time the crypt, part of the apse, the **Nativity Façade** and one tower were finished. His tomb lies in the crypt. In 1936, many of the plans were destroyed in the civil war, although enough remained to continue the work in 1957. The present towers were finished in 1975.

Today the site is chaotic with cranes and building materials as construction continues amid some contro-versy. One faction believes the project should be left as it is, in tribute to Gaudí, while others are determined to see it completed. There are already rumblings about architect Jordi Bonet's stark interpretation of the **Passion Façade**, including giant sculptures by Josep María Subirachs, which Gaudí devotees complain is too far removed from the architect's style. Whatever your opinion, this fascinating church is a must on any tour of Barcelona owing to its sheer originality and architectural genius.

Touring the Sagrada Família

In the entrance, a scale model demonstrates the breathtaking proportions of the finished product. There will be 18 towers: 12 for the Apostles (eight of which have been built); four for the Evangelists; one for the Virgin and a massive, 170m (558ft) spire topped by a lamb symbolizing Christ. Three dramatic façades will represent nativity, passion and glory and the Temple itself will hold 5550 worshippers. Visitors can take the lift 112m (367ft) up one of the spires and walk onto a narrow concrete bridge, dizzyingly high above the city. Real enthusiasts can climb up even higher on a stone, spiral staircase.

The Nativity Façade

Back on solid ground, the nativity façade currently appears to be the back of the Temple although it will actually form a side of the finished building. Gaudí wanted this façade to face east, so the sunrise would bring new life to the miracle of birth every morning.

All kinds of stories are told on the façade, the detail of which is best studied through binoculars. The turtle and tortoise at the base represent the care that was taken with the work, as well as the water and the earth of the Creation. Further up, crustaceans symbolize eternity. Various biblical scenes are

GAUDÍ

For all his glory in his native town, Gaudí's work is hardly featured outside Catalunya. He has, however, produced a few works in other parts of Spain. In 1903 he was commissioned to restructure the interior of the magnificent cathedral in Palma. In Santander, he designed a country house for the brother-in-law of the Marquis of Comillas with a minaret-like circular tower. There are also two Gaudi buildings in Leon, a house designed for Güell's friends, and a spectacular Bishop's Palace in Astorga, which looks like a small castle.

Below: *Grandiose in conception, the Sagrada Família is no less magnificent in its detail.*

depicted, from the coronation of the Virgin to the appearance of the angel Gabriel; the Three Wise Men and shepherds in the fields, and the flight from Egypt. The passage of the stars through the sky is also detailed. Look out for the copper trumpets and the bow of the violinist being held by the angels. The caves, clouds and ice were all inspired by rock formations at Montserrat, a spectacular monastery and shrine amid the dramatic mountain scenery which is within driving distance of Barcelona.

Museu de la Sagrada Família

Under the site, the small cathedral museum follows the history of the building and explains the method behind Gaudí's work. Models and diagrams explain his previously untested theories of architecture, and sketches and plaster models show his painstaking methods of creating the statues that adorn the nativity façade. This involved taking plaster casts of the bodies of those friends and neighbours whom, he believed, most resembled the biblical characters he wanted to portray. He would then use real skeletons to examine the movement of the human body before making the statues. Open 10:00–14:00, 16:00–19:00 daily.

Hospital de la Santa Creu i de Sant Pau *

At the opposite end of the Avinguda de Gaudí is the University Hospital, quite unlike any other medical establishment. Built between 1902 and 1912 by Gaudí's contemporary Domènech i Montaner, the building consists of a series of pavilions clad in colourful ceramics and domes, set in beautiful, tranquil gardens. Domènech's son Pere oversaw the completion of the building in 1930, which was seven years after his father's death.

Parc Güell

The fantasy of banker Eusebio Güell, this city oasis, which is 15 minutes' walk from Plaça des Lesseps metro, was intended to be an exclusive housing estate. Güell bought a plot of land on the slopes of the **Muntanya Pelada** at the fringe of the Eixample in 1899 and commissioned Antoni Gaudí to design an estate of 60 houses, each with a garden.

The development never took off and only the foundations and two houses were built. What remains today is a beautiful park with sweeping views of the city below and some extraordinary architectural features. The park has been open to the public since 1922 and is protected by UNESCO as a world heritage site. In 1969 it was declared a historical monument and the house was founded by the Friends of Gaudí in 1963.

In order to preserve the beauty of the mountainside, Gaudí built three curved viaducts so that the roads would follow the natural contours. Most of the existing vegetation was kept: orange trees, firs, carobs, olives and prickly pear, with

Barcelona's Metro is fast, efficient and clean, its five lines radiating out from the Plaça de Catalunya. Travelling underground avoids the often cougested streets and is a quick and easy way to get around the city. The most cost efficient way to do this is to buy a block of ten tickets, either from a machine or from the attendant. One type covers the Metro and buses, while a second, cheaper version covers just the Metro and the regional FF.CC service to Tibidabo. Platforms and trains are well lit and usually busy, although women and single travellers should consider using a taxi late at night.

Above: *Symbols of the dragon appear all over Barcelona. Gaudí's Parc Güell is no exception.*
Below: *Yet more Gaudí – he designed Parc Güell as a luxury housing estate for his patron Eusebio Güell.*

pink almond blossoms and the heavy aroma of wild sage, thyme and rosemary scenting the air in springtime.

The most striking feature of the park is the marketplace. Two colourful pavilions flank the entrance to the park and a flight of steps, guarded by a large, rainbow-coloured dragon, lead up to a market square. Underneath, 86 columns create a gallery effect where the market stalls would have been, but today are curiously empty. Thousands of white, broken mosaic patterns across a contoured ceiling give the impression of billowing clouds.

On top is one of Gràcia's favourite gathering places. Surrounding the main square is the amazing '**wave bench**', one continuous stone bench decked in countless fragments of coloured mosaic, undulating around the edges. Barcelona stretches out below, and at weekends the place is packed with people reading the paper and picnicking, as well as art students sketching the mosaics. A couple of cafés are set into the rock face in man-made grottoes. Higher up the hillside are children's play areas facing west to Tibidado and a small *petanca* square where old men gather for a heated debate over the game.

Casa Museu Gaudí *

In the centre of the park is the show home in which Gaudí lived in 1906 when he was designing the park. Gaudí did not actually design this house but he lived there from 1906 till 1926. Inside, the house is disappointingly austere; Gaudí was deeply religious and lived a spartan life. There are, however, a few *modernista* gems, a mirror with an elaborate gilt frame, a few pieces of furniture and some extravagant fabric samples. Open 10:00–14:00 and 16:00–19:00, Monday–Friday, 10:00–14:00, Sundays.

GRÀCIA

Once a small village on the plains between Tibidado and the Mediterranean, Gràcia has been swallowed up by the tentacles of the city. Home of the liberal and artistic community in the last century, Gràcia retains an independent spirit and, with its narrow streets and pretty squares, has a real village atmosphere, particularly during festivals, when garlands deck the streets. Some of the city's best restaurants and bars are found here and a trip on a summer's night is most rewarding.

There are a few sights, notably **Casa Vicens**, one of Gaudí's first designs, built for a tile maker in 1883. Unlike Gaudí's later work, the house is geometric in design with strong Mudéjar influences, and orange and blue tiles adorn the exterior.

In the heart of Gràcia, in the tower of Plaça de Ruis i Taulet, is the **Campana de Gràcia** – the Gràcia bell. In 1870, during a revolt against taxes, the bell was tolled incessantly and could be heard in Barcelona.

Also worth stopping for is the **Plaça del Sol**, packed with life on a hot summer's night as locals gather round the outside tables before moving on to Gràcia's many clubs and restaurants. During the day, the square is a great spot for people watching.

SHERRY DRINKING

Sherry is a national institution in Spain, though always produced in Andalucía in the south, is drunk everywhere. In addition to *fino*, there are three types of sherry drunk in Spain. *Manzanilla* is a type of dry *fino* with a salty tang, acquired from grapes grown around the Andalucían coastal town of Sanlucar de Barrameda. *Amontillado*, meanwhile, is a more pungent wine that has been aged beyond its normal span in the bodega, while *oloroso*, the heaviest style of sherry, is usually sweetened and sold as cream exclusively to the British market.

Left: *Plaça del Sol is the main meeting place in Gràcia.*
Opposite: *Locals gather to read the Sunday papers on Gaudi's wave bench.*

6
Montjuïc

Montjuïc is Barcelona's playground, a rocky, wooded headland jutting out south of the city above the docks where local people jog, walk their dogs and generally enjoy the fresh air and sweeping views of the city below.

In many ways, Montjuïc is made for entertainment. On one hand, it is cloaked in shady woods interspersed with botanical gardens and occasional glimpses of the blue Mediterranean, while on the other, it's packed with cultural interest. Many of the buildings were constructed for the 1929 Expo, hence the rather theatrical appearance of the area. There's the magnificently opulent neoclassical **Palau Nacional**, dramatically lit at night; excellent museums; the **Poble Espanyol** (a village recreating architectural styles from all over Spain); the **Olympic Stadium** and, right at the other end of the cultural spectrum, a funfair. A highlight for many is the stunning **Miró Foundation**, a superb collection of the artist's work in a dazzling setting.

Montjuïc's past, however, has been less than entertaining. Because of its strategic position, the 'mountain of the Jews' played an important role for whoever controlled the city. Once a Jewish cemetery, the summit has been occupied by a fortress since the Middle Ages and the present **castle**, which hides its own grisly secrets, was built in the mid-18th century.

Montjuïc merits a full day out and even getting there is part of the fun. A **funicular** railway runs from the Paral.lel metro station, but in summer many people take the scenic route, a dizzying **cable car** ride from the harbour.

DON'T MISS

*** Joan Miró Foundation: beautifully designed modern museum housing some of the artist's best paintings and sculptures.
*** Palau Nacional: one of the world's great medieval art collections.
*** Olympic Stadium: scene of all the action in the 1992 Olympic Games.
** Museu Militar: reminders of Catalunya's bloody past in a dramatic cliff top setting.

Opposite: *Montjuïc affords spectacular views of the city.*

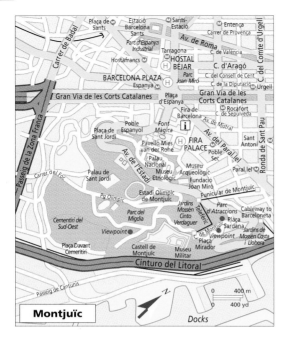

Montjuïc

Plaça d'Espanya ★★

The metro steps here emerge into another world. **Avinguda de La Reina Maria Cristina** is flanked by two imposing obelisks modelled on the San Marco tower in Venice. These guard the entrance to the **fairground**, dramatically laid out by Puig i Cadafalch, and a series of spectacular pavilions constructed for Barcelona's second **Expo** in 1929, today used for trade fairs. Brilliant red-and-yellow Catalan flags flutter in the breeze. Straight ahead is the opulent **Palau Nacional**, reached by an enormous flight of steps, illuminated after dark by dazzling white spotlights fanning out into the night sky behind the Palace. In front, the **Font Màgica** (magic fountain) sprays 3000 jets of water backlit by rainbow colours every night, with musical accompaniment at weekends. The fountain is currently closed for repairs but the floodlit Palace is still worth a visit en route to the Poble Espanyol, now one of Barcelona's most fashionable nightspots.

Pavelló Mies van der Rohe ★

Built by the German architect Mies van der Rohe for the Expo in 1929, the pavilion, which was the reception area for the exhibition, was dismantled after the event and put back together again by a group of Catalan architects in 1986. Smooth, polished surfaces of bottle-green onyx and clear glass create a cool, restful atmosphere around a pool. The building is currently used as a study centre. Open 10:00–18:00, daily.

THE SARDANA

The national dance of Catalunya is supposed to be an expression of Catalan independence. The dance can be performed by any number of people, all of whom put an object in the middle (to symbolize sharing) and join hands. A strange orchestra known as the *copla*, usually consisting of flute, drums and oboes, accompanies the dancers. The Sardana is performed in front of the cathedral every Sunday at 10:00; in the Plaça de Catalunya on Sunday morning and in the Plaça de Sant Jaume on Sunday at 18:00.

PALAU NACIONAL

Reaching the Palau Nacional has been made much easier now that giant escalators have been built on either side of the long flights of steps leading up to the building. The Palau Nacional was supposed to have been dismantled in 1934 but gained a reprieve and became home to one of the most impressive collections of medieval art in the world, now the **Museu d'Art de Catalunya**. Open 09:00–21:00, daily.

The Romanesque section consists of room after room of magnificent frescoes, all from tiny churches dating back 1000 years, high in the Pyrenees. The frescoes, most of which portray biblical scenes, were removed for their protection around 1920, the reason being that the churches were lying abandoned. Some of the best known works include the apse from the church of Santa María de Taüll, with a scene of David and Goliath, and the 1123 masterpiece of Pantocràtor from Sant Climent de Taüll. A notable feature of these 1000-year-old frescoes is their astonishingly brilliant colours.

The Gothic collection includes church pieces and tombs as well as paintings, representing the best of Catalan art with work by, among others, Jaume Huguet. Spanish greats such as Velázquez and El Greco are represented in the later Baroque and Renaissance rooms.

MORE MIRÓ

Miró's influence is firmly imprinted on Barcelona and can be spotted in the most unlikely places. The ceramic walls at the airport are a Miró design; he also designed the logo for the Spanish Tourist Board and the blue and red starfish of the Caixe de Pensions. Stroll down the Rambla and you'll walk over the huge Miró mosaic on the pavement at Plaça de la Boquería. Also visit the Parc Joan Miró in the northern Eixample to see the famous Dona i Ocell (woman and bird) sculpture in the lake.

Below: *Cascading fountains in front of the Palau Nacional.*

FUNDACIÓ JOAN MIRÓ

Acknowledged as one of Barcelona's best museums, the
building of the Miró foundation is as much a joy as the
contents. A stark, white structure with huge windows,
designed by **Josep-Luis Sert**, a friend of Miró's, is set
around tranquil gardens. Sun filters through the trees and
casts splashes of light on the brilliantly coloured paintings
and tapestries offset by the minimalist style of the rooms.

The museum was opened in 1975, although Miró
formed the Joan Miró foundation in 1971 with his
friend, **Joan Prats**. The foundation was a private
cultural venture with two objectives: to provide a centre
for the study of Miró's work and to promote contemporary and avant-garde art.

There are two main sections: the Miró collection itself,
a mixture of sculptures, paintings and textiles, and the
'To Joan Miró' room where the works of Miró's contemporaries are displayed, all donated as a gesture of their
admiration of the artist and his work. Miró died in

Mallorca in 1983; the building was
extended in 1986 to accommodate its
growing activities.

In the Miró section, the first exhibits
are enormous textiles: giant woven rugs
in the stunning primary colours that were
Miró's trademark. His paintings and
drawings show a childlike delight in
colour and form – bold strokes, delicate
lines and colourful spots. Outside, on the
flat roof, visitors can wander around a
collection of his bizarre sculptures, displayed at their very best in the right
sunlight. One of the most poignant
exhibits, however, is the Barcelona series
from 1939–44, black and white litho-
graphs displayed on a bright yellow wall.
Like all his contemporaries, Miró
expressed his horror at the Spanish Civil
War through his work, in this instance
with dark figures and distorted faces.

Left: *Views are spectacular from everywhere on Montjuïc.*
Opposite: *Miró's metal sculptures are displayed on the roof of the Fundació Joan Miró to show off their dazzling colours.*

Another highlight of this section, though not by Miró, is Alexander Calder's famous **Mercury Fountain**, which was designed in 1937 for the Spanish government's pavilion at the Paris Expo. Calder described the work as 'an attempt to bring movement to sculpture' and the fountain is certainly mesmerizing as mercury streams around it in silver rivers, safely housed behind glass.

The now permanent collection, A Joan Miró, forms the second section of the museum and contains a fabulous assortment of work donated by, among others, **Matisse**, **Henry Moore**, **Angel Ferrant**, **Richard Serra** and **Antoni Tàpies**, all friends of the artist.

Also fascinating is the room of Miró's sketches and life drawings; anyone with even a remote interest in art will enjoy the jottings on restaurant menus and bits of newspaper that metamorphosed into million-dollar masterpieces.

There's a pleasant café at the foundation as well as a rather stylish souvenir shop, where Miró merchandizing goes to town. In addition to the usual books, posters, hats and T-shirts, you can buy Miró umbrellas, crockery, hanging mobiles, notebooks and even caramels wrapped in Miró paper. The foundation is also an important centre for contemporary classical music, and hosts a series of concerts in summer. Open 11:00–19:00, Tuesday, Wednesday, Friday, Saturday, 11:00–21:30, Thursday, 10:30–14:30, Sunday.

BARCELONA FOR FREE

Travelling on a budget is rewarding in Barcelona as many of the attractions are free. You can visit the Olympic Stadium; peer into the cool depths of the cathedral; admire the buildings and the Park Güell by Gaudí; inspect the museums of graphic art, coins, ethnography and perfume; poke around the Boquería market, enjoy the street entertainment in the Rambla; and window shop in the design emporium Vinçon, virtually a museum in itself.

Right: *A visit to the archaeological museum is worthwhile before exploring historical Catalunya.*

Museu Etnològic and Museu Arqueològic *

The ethnological museum, a varied collection of pieces from Africa, Japan, Central and South America is housed behind the Palau Nacional in a stark, modern building, also a relic from the Expo. The archaeological museum is more pertinent to Barcelona, with a good, in-depth study of the background of Catalunya. Exhibits covering the Costa Brava to the Balearics, span history from the palaeolithic (the emergence of primitive man and the manufacture of stone tools) to the Visigothic period, including ceramics, mosaics and sculptures from the Greek and Roman periods. There's even a reconstruction of a Roman funeral chamber of the sort that can be found in the ancient sites of Andalucía. If you plan to visit the Roman remains at Empúries on the **Costa Brava**, then it is important to visit this museum as it gives a good background to the site. Both museums are open 10:00–14:00, but hours are 10:00–19:00 on Tuesdays and Thursdays.

Just outside is an open-air **Greek theatre**, also built for the Expo and set in an old stone quarry (many buildings around Barcelona are made from Montjuïc stone), now used for summer drama festivals. Other Expo buildings have also been put to good use: the **Palau Albéniz** in the lovely old Jardins de Joan Maragall contains a small fresco by **Salvador Dalí** and is used to accommodate visiting dignitaries, while the **Mercat de les Flors**, once a flower market, is now a theatre.

OLYMPIC VENUES

The venues for the 1992 Olympic Games were built intentionally equidistant from one another in the four corners of the city and linked by a new bypass, the Rondes. The Olympic Village and the marina where the yachting events took place are northeast of the centre, while the main stadium on Montjuïc is in the southeast. Roughly southwest, around Pedralbes, are huge tennis court complexes and the football stadium of Camp Nou and in the northwest, a new Velodrome was constructed at Vall d'Hebron to host the cycling events.

Poble Espanyol **

Yet another showcase from the Expo, the **Spanish Village** faithfully reproduces the country's architecture and customs in its streets and squares. After a facelift in 1992, the village has become a popular place for locals as well as tourists with its Basque-style houses and the narrow streets and whitewashed Andalucían quarter. All sorts of craft workshops provide added entertainment and there's even a mini glass blowing factory.

The village is, of course, uninhabited, but since Barcelona's hottest design team, Alfredo Arribas and Xavier Mariscal, were brought in to spice the place up, the main square, **Plaça Major,** has become a magnet on hot summer nights, buzzing with outdoor bars and cafés, and clubbers moving on to the futuristic **Torre d'Avila** nightclub after midnight. There's even a **flamenco** *tablao* (club) for more traditional Spanish entertainment.

> ### CASTELL DE MONTJUÏC
>
> Montjuïc's Castell served as a military prison for many years. During the Spanish Civil War it was commandeered by Franco to serve as a local interrogation centre and it was deep in the castle's bowels, in 1940, that he ordered the Guardia Civil to execute Lluís Companys, then President of Catalunya.
>
> In 1960 Franco returned the castle to the city, which showed its 'gratitude' in a huge stone monument, visible from the battlements.

OLYMPIC STADIUM

Barcelona's Olympic Stadium is perched high on the rocky mass of Montjuïc with the city and the sparkling Mediterranean stretched out below. The stadium itself was actually constructed for the 1929 Expo and was intended to be used for the 'people's' alternative to the Nazi-dominated 1936 Olympics in Berlin. These never, in fact, took place as the Spanish Civil War broke out before the stadium was even opened.

A new team of Catalan architects was brought in to modernize the stadium for the 1992 Games, although the 1929 façade was retained. To create a classical-style stadium, the arena's original base was sunk 12m (39ft) into the ground to accommodate 65,000 spectators. Free tours take place between 10:00 and 18:00 daily.

Below: *The original 1929 façade was kept on the new Olympic Stadium.*

Above: *This statue on Montjuïc commemorates the Sardana, Catalunya's national dance.*
Opposite: *The tower of Montjuïc castle made an ideal lookout for approaching enemy ships.*

NIGHTLIFE WITH A DIFFERENCE

The Avinguda Paral.lel is the centre of Barcelona's music hall society with raunchy, Parisian-style shows taking place in theatres like **El Molino**, the **Teatre Arnau** and the **Teatre Apolo**. More sophisticated variety theatre takes place at the **Belle Epoque**. Alternatively, ballroom dancing is alive and well in Barcelona with several grand old venues holding regular classes and sessions in foxtrot, tango and salsa. Try **La Paloma**, **Envelat** and **Bolero**, three of the most fashionable. See the *Guía del Ocio* for details.

Palau de Sant Jordi ★★

In contrast to the neoclassical grandeur of the stadium, Japanese architect Arata Isozaki's Palau de Sant Jordi is a piece of science fiction, a sleek, low-lying dome in silver and black. Holding 17,000 spectators, it is one of the largest sports halls in the world. The stone-and-metal 'forest' sculpture outside is the work of the architect's wife, Aiko Miyawaki.

Galeria Olimpica ★

At the south gate of the stadium, this museum features video footage from the 1992 Olympic Games as well as memorabilia from the games where several world records were set. For true Olympic fans, there's a library and information centre as well. Open 10:00–14:00, 16:00–20:00 Tuesday–Saturday, 10:00–14:00, Sunday.

Parc d'Atraccions ★★

This is Barcelona's second mountain-top amusement park which provides a great day out for children. There are around 40 rides, including a ferris wheel and a roller coaster. A second cable car goes from here up to the castle; alternatively, a path winds it way up the hill past the Mirador de l'Alcalde, a great place from which to soak up the breathtaking view of the docks and city below. Open 16:30–20:15 daily, 16:30–24:00, Saturday–Sunday.

On the way is the **Sardana Memorial**, a life-sized sculpture by Catalan artist Josep Canyas depicting figures performing Catalunya's national dance. There are two more sets of ornamental gardens in this corner of Montjuïc: the **Jardins Mossén Cinto Vergaduer** below the castle and the tropical **Jardins Mossén Costa i Llobera** on the sunny, protected southeast slopes of the mountain.

CASTELL DE MONTJUÏC
Museu Militar ★★

The excellent military museum is housed in the Castell de Montjuïc, an 18th-century fortress built on 17th-century ruins on the top of Montjuïc. The museum is all the more atmospheric for its setting within the damp stone walls. Old weapons, military uniforms and medals evoke images of the prisoners taken by Felipe V in the 18th century, and of the Republicans who were imprisoned in the dungeon during the civil war. Open 09:30–13:30, 15:30–19:30, Tuesday–Sunday.

ROAD SIGNS
Aduana • customs
Autopista (de peaje) • Motorway/highway (toll)
Ceda el paso • Give way
Circunvalación • ring road or bypass
Cruce peligroso • dangerous crossroads
Despacio • slow
Desviación • diversion
Entrada • entrance
Obras • workmen
Prohibido adelantar • no overtaking
Estacionamento prohibido • no parking
Sin plomo • unleaded petrol
Salida • exit
Salida de camiones • lorry exit
Puesto de soccoro • first aid post

POBLE SEC

Graffitied steps lead down through neglected scrubland on the side of Montjuïc to Poble Sec, a fairly undesirable area, once an industrial estate, now bordering the Barri Xines. Separating the two, however, the broad **Avinguda del Paral.lel** is a hive of activity at night, packed with cinemas and cabaret theatres, one of which, El Molino, has been a city highlight for years. Refer to the *Guía del Ocio* for listings of events here and at the city's other theatres.

The name Paral.lel, incidentally, comes from the astronomer Comas i Solà, who discovered that the avenue coincided exactly with the parallel 41 to 44 degrees North.

7
Greater Barcelona

With such a concentration of spectacular buildings in the centre of the city, it's all too easy to miss those scattered around the outskirts. But the former villages of **Horta** and **Sarria** are well worth a visit, where what would merely be the leafy lanes of suburbia in another country are striking, broad avenues lined with miniature castles, mostly constructed around the turn of the century as the city was expanding.

At weekends head for Barcelona's playground, **Tibidabo**, part of the pine-clad Collserola mountain range that forms a natural backdrop to the sea. The views are breathtaking and the air clean. There are other green areas to explore too, such as the beautiful **labyrinth** at Horta and the **Parc de la Creueta del Coll**, a tiny, man-made swimming lake with a beach.

Southwest of the city are some lovely old buildings. A visit to the **Pedralbes** monastery is like stepping back in time into the silent world of the nuns who lived there for hundreds of years. The **Palau Reial**, meanwhile, is set in peaceful parkland north of the Diagonal. It boasts wonderful furniture, sculptures and paintings; its park includes a formal garden.

South of the highway some of the city's most avant garde experimentation with *nou urbanisme* took place, resulting in ultra-modern parks with giant sculptures and futuristic fountains. Here, too, is the home of the legendary soccer team **FC Barcelona**, or Barca; the cheers of the 120,000-strong crowd can be heard from miles around on a match day.

Don't Miss

** **Tibidabo:** a trip up Barcelona's mountain for sweeping views of the city.
** **Monastir de Pedralbes:** beautiful old monastery in a tranquil setting.
* **Palau Reial:** neoclassical palace on the city's outskirts housing a ceramic museum.
* **Museu de Futbol:** a chance to visit the great Camp Nou.
* **Laberint d'Horta:** strange labyrinth in a beautiful park.

Opposite: *The grid pattern of the Eixample is clearly visible from Tibidabo.*

Right: *Barcelona's pristine
but ancient blue tram
ferries visitors to the
Tibidabo funicular.*

TIBIDABO

The highest point of the pine-clad hills that encircle the
city is the mountain of Tibidabo, a towering 550m
(1805ft), from which the views are legendary. On a rare
pollution-free day with the right atmospheric conditions,
people claim to be able to see as far as the Balearic
Islands, 128km (80 miles) out to sea.

At weekends, local people flock to the hills to visit the
excellent amusement park on Tibidabo, have a picnic
and generally enjoy the fresh air. Getting there by public
transport is an adventure in itself. From the Plaça de
Catalunya, take the FGC train to the Tibidabo stop. The
heart of a rich suburb, its broad streets are lined with
noblemen's houses built at the turn of the century, when
Barcelona was expanding.

An antique tram, the **Tramvia Blau**, creaks and
grinds its way up the hill to the Tibidabo funicular,
smartly decked out in shiny, navy blue paint and highly
polished wood. First, though, look at the building on the
corner by the tram stop, **La Rotunda**, an amazingly fussy
modernista structure with a domed roof. Once a dance
hall and brothel, it now serves as a hospital.

From the top of the tram line, take the funicular up
the mountainside. At the top, there is a whole new world
of entertainment as well as a couple of bars and restaurants with outdoor terraces offering a marvellous
bird's-eye view of the city.

Left: *The lavish Sagrat Cor church is a popular spot for weddings.*

El Sagrat Cor de Jesus ★

Dominating the summit of Tibidabo is a church, designed by **Enric Sagnier** at the turn of the century and completed by his son in 1952 after the civil war. The two parts of the church are almost like two separate buildings. A neo-Romanesque nave with some extravagant *modernista* features forms the base while the section above is neo-Gothic with a 4.8 tonne, 7½m (25ft) statue of Christ, arms outstretched like the famous statue in Rio de Janeiro. With its dramatic setting, it's no surprise that this church is very popular for weddings. Open 08:00–19:00 daily.

Parc d'Atraccions del Tibidabo ★★

Barcelona's main amusement park perches precariously on the edge of the mountainside, giving the adrenalin-boosting illusion on some of the rides that the carriages really are flying 520m (1706ft) above the ground. The rides include everything from a roller coaster to children's roundabouts and some unusual features like a rotating vintage aeroplane, dating back to 1928. A miniature train suspended from a monorail circles the park over some hair-raising drops. A little museum inside the park, the **Museu d'Autòmates del Tibidabo**, contains slot machines and mechanical toys from the 19th and 20th centuries. Park open 17:00–02:00, Monday–Thursday, 17:00–03:00, Friday–Saturday, 12:00–23:00, Sunday; in winter 12:00–20:00 weekends only.

TORRE COLLSEROLA

Two unusual buildings can be seen on the hillside from Tibidabo. The dome-shaped structure is the Observatori Fabra, built in 1907 and used for meteorological, seismic and atomic research. Between Tibidabo and the next mountain is a giant, futuristic telecommunications tower, Torre Collserola, designed by British architect Sir Norman Foster. A glass elevator glides up the 288m (945ft) structure to a spectacular mirador, pricy but worth it for another amazing view of the city. A shuttle bus runs to the tower from the top of the funicular.

Parc de Collserola *

Essentially part of the same range of hills as Tibidabo, the mountain to the south also has a funicular which leads from the city outskirts to **Vallvidrera**, currently one of the most exclusive suburbs of Barcelona. Mountain bikes can be hired here and several walking trails are marked, although it's best to call at the tourist board for a map before setting out.

Wildlife thrives in the city's green lung: red squirrels, wild boar, foxes and the rare genet live under the shade of the broom and pine trees while birds inhabiting the area include the hoopoe, Eleanora's falcon, the spotted eagle and bee-eaters.

FINCA GÜELL

Beyond the palace is a large, grassy park, the Parc de Pedralbes, with Barcelona's University buildings on its fringes. At the far end of the park is the Finca Güell, the former stables of the wealthy Güell family, whose land stretched from here some distance south of the Diagonal. Gaudí was commissioned to build the porter's house, the gate and the stable pavilions, which are decked out in bright blue and white tiles. The only part of the estate visible to the public is the wrought iron gate with its menacing dragon, which raises its claws when the gate is open.

Museu de la Ciència *

Missing the city's Science Museum would be imposs-ible as its name on the hillside of Tibidabo rivals the Hollywood sign in Los Angeles. What's more, a model of a World War II submarine sits in the middle of the road outside the building.

Inside, the museum takes a very modern, hands-on approach with all sorts of buttons to press. A series of galleries includes waves, vision, the living planet, mechanics and meteorology. For an extra fee, visit the Planetarium, where the night sky in brilliant detail is projected onto a dome 10m (33ft) wide. Another part of the museum, specially designed by Javier Mariscal and Alfredo Arribas, is set aside for small children to play away to their hearts' content with fascinating scientific objects. Parents are not admitted to this haven of experimentation, but monitors are there to keep watch over the children. Open 10:00–20:00, Tuesday–Sunday.

PEDRALBES

Like the suburbs of Sarria and Horta, Pedralbes, the northern side of the western Diagonal, is an old-monied neighbourhood of dignified streets and stately houses. There are several sights here, enough to merit a day if you take in the unlikely combination of a Gaudí house, a Gothic monastery, a neoclassical Palace and the football museum to the south.

Palau Reial de Pedralbes *

Barcelona's Royal Palace is surrounded by ornamental gardens with pools and statues. The Palace was constructed at the order of King Alfonso XIII between 1919 and 1924, as there was nowhere in the city at the time considered suitable for royal functions. The Palace was built by extending a stately home belonging to the Güell family. Inevitably, Franco used the building for his own purposes during the civil war. Open 10:00–18:00 daily in winter, 10:00–20:00 in summer.

Opposite: *The Science Museum has plenty of working exhibits.*

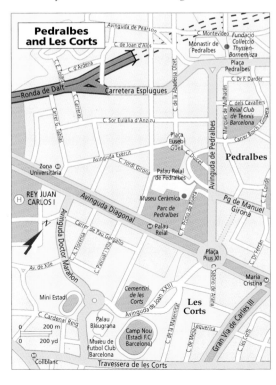

Museu Ceràmica *

Inside the Palace is the ceramic museum, which was transferred here from the Palau Nacional on Montjuïc. Ranging from the late 12th century to the present, the collection traces the history of glazed Spanish ceramics. Contemporary designs by Picasso, Miró, Artigas and Cumella are also on display. Open 10:00–17:00, Tuesday–Sunday.

Monastir de Pedralbes **

Heading towards the hills, this beautiful Gothic monastery is located at the end of the Avinguda Pedralbes. A cluster of medieval buildings in a good state of repair, the monastery was founded in 1326 by Queen Elisenda de Montcada, the last wife of King Jaume II. Nuns of the order of St Clare have lived here since the 14th century and a wander through the old refectory (communal dining hall), kitchens and herb garden gives a fascinating insight into their lives.

The cloisters, however, are the monastery's most exquisite feature, three levels of passageways supported by impossibly slender columns, with a Renaissance fountain at the centre. Frescoes and religious artefacts are stored in the gallery around the cloister.

The church dates back to 1419 and contains the marble tomb of Queen Elisenda, who lived here for the last 30 years of her life. A simple design with a single aisle, the church retains some of its original stained glass windows. There's also a small chapel, dedicated to Sant

Miquel and decorated with ornate paintings from around 1345 by the Catalan artist Ferrer Bassa. Open 10:00–17:00, Tuesday–Saturday, 10:00–14:00, Sunday.

Fundació Collecció Thyssen-Bornemisza **

Some 71 paintings and eight sculptures from the private collection of Baron Thyssen Bornemisza are displayed in one of the monastery's old dormitories. Spanning 600 years, the collection includes work by Titian, Rubens and Tintoretto with examples of Italian Baroque, late Venetian Baroque and some Spanish pieces by Velázquez. The remainder of the collection is in the Villahermosa Palace in Madrid. Open 10:00–14:00, Tuesday–Sunday.

Left: *FC Barcelona proudly displays its trophies in the football museum.*
Opposite: *Medieval walls on Pedralbes' ancient monastery.*

NEW BARCELONA

South of the western Diagonal, the district known as Les Corts was the scene of extensive building before the Olympics, glassy towers emerging along the main cross streets to house designer shops and hi tech offices. The new university is here, as well as the **Camp Nou** football stadium – home of the legendary FC Barcelona. A couple of five-star hotels and most recently, a new convention centre have sprung up around the tennis club and polo club, effectively making this area a mini-financial and business hub, shifting the emphasis away from the old city centre. With the exception of a couple of interesting architectural sites and the Football Museum, this district is fairly removed from the tourist trail; it is considered fashionable to live here now.

Museu de Futbol Club Barcelona *

Even the most reluctant visitor will recognize some of the names in this museum's glittering hall of fame, which includes England's Gary Lineker and Argentina's Maradona. Set inside the vast Camp Nou football stadium, which dwarfs the Olympic Stadium with its 120,000 capacity, the museum charts a history of Spain's most famous team, FC Barcelona, over the last century. The museum includes a visit to the VIP box,

SPANISH SPORTING STARS

The fact that tennis, golf and cycling are national passions in Spain is no surprise, given the success of Spanish sporting stars in these fields. Arantxa Sánchez Vicario, Conchita Martinez and Alberto Berasategui dominate the international tennis circuit, while Seve Ballesteros and José Maria Olazábel are two of the world's great golfers. Miguel Indurain, meanwhile, is a national hero for his multiple wins of the Tour de France and visitors to Catalunya will often have to make way on the mountain roads for groups of racing cyclists speeding along in emulation.

Above: Nou urbanisme *in the futuristic Parc d'Espanya Industrial.*

from which it is possible to appreciate the sheer size of the stadium. Matches take place most Sundays and while tickets are like gold dust they are worth fighting for to experience the atmosphere of 120,000 roaring fans. Open 10:00–18:30, Monday–Saturday; 10:00–24:00, Sunday and holidays.

Parc d'Espanya Industrial ★

Throughout the city, attempts have been made to incorporate modern art into everyday urban areas, a movement known as *nou urbanisme*. One of the most impressive examples is the **Parc d'Espanya Industrial**, a post-modernist recreational park south of the football stadium next to Sants, the main railway station.

Designed by Basque architects Luis Penya Canchegui and Francesc Rius i Camps, the park showcases the work of six sculptors. These sculptures range from the classical period to avant-garde. The thinking behind it was to create a modern interpretation of a Roman bath, with a central boating lake surrounded by steps. The whole scene is overlooked by 10 futuristic 'lighthouses' in a modern industrial design with yellow and red candy-striped tops. The most striking sculpture is the inevitable St George's Dragon (Drac de Sant Jordi) by Andrés Nagel, in this case an iron monster incorporating a children's slide.

MORE MODERN ARCHITECTURE

Serious followers of modern architecture may like to seek out the following:
Parc del Clot: Modern park in the Clot district incorporating a disused railway and old chimney; notable for the sculpture, *The Rites of Spring*, by American Bryan Hunt.
Parc de la Pegaso: Park in the district of La Sagrera on the site of a former factory, featuring a paved square and a sculpture by Ellsworth Kelly.
Via Júlia: a long, Rambla-type promenade in the Verdum district with two modern sculptures.
Sculpture-bridge: Linking Sant Andreu and El Poble Nou, this graceful road bridge was designed by architect and engineer Santiago Calatrava.

Parc Joan Miró *

Close by, on the site of an old abattoir is the Parc Joan Miró, so called because of the artist's famous **Dona i Ocell** statue, a huge, brilliantly coloured model of a woman and bird, which rises to 22m (70ft) and adorns the centre of a pool. Although the park is small, it is popular with local people and there are games areas, grass to lie on and a small café.

HORTA
Laberint d'Horta *

Lying at the foot of the Collserola hills is the village of Horta which was once famous for its invigorating atmosphere and is still the location of various health-related institutions. Worth seeing here is the site of a former 14th-century monastery, **Vall d'Hebron**, now replaced by a mansion built in 1799 by the Marquises

Below: *'Woman and Bird' in the Parc Joan Miró.*

d'Alfarràs, set in pleasant gardens dotted with interesting mythological statues. The building today houses the School of Restoration.

Now a public park, the central feature of the estate is a magnificent labyrinth of cypress hedges in which it is very easy to get lost. Anyone meeting this fate has to wait to be rescued at sunset when the park keepers come round blowing on their whistles. Just below the park is the **Velodrome.**

Parc de la Creueta de Coll *

West of Horta, just north of the Parc Güell, is an unusual park designed by the architects responsible for the Olympic Village, featuring a swimming lake reclaimed from an old quarry. An enormous stone sculpture, **Elogi de l'Aigua** (eulogy to water) by Basque artist Eduardo Chillida, is suspended by steel cables over the water.

8
Excursions from Barcelona

Beyond Barcelona, a fascinating hinterland waits to be explored. To the south, the golden beaches of the **Costa Daurada** extend all the way to the city of **Tarragona**, the rolling hills and fields inland lined with endless grape vines. An easy trip from the city is to the cellars of **Sant Sadurní**, heart of the sparkling wine producing area, or to the town of **Vilafranca del Penedès**, where some of the country's best still whites are produced.

High spot on the Costa Daurada for partygoers is **Sitges**, a flamboyant holiday resort with a colourful community that arrives for the summer. For families, **Port Aventura** is a better bet, Spain's biggest and most technically advanced theme park, where a day watching the street entertainers, riding the roller coasters and sampling food from all over the world soon passes.

Inland from Barcelona, the most important excursion is to the **Montserrat** mountain, a vast chunk of wind-eroded limestone that has been a shrine for over 1000 years. To the north, the beaches of the Costa Brava beckon, a string of sandy bays interspersed with pine woods and jagged cliffs, forming one of Spain's most beautiful coastlines. At the northern end of the coast, the eccentric **Salvador Dalí Museum** in Figueres is the main attraction while inland, the lovely medieval city of **Girona** and the mountain principality of Andorra merit at least a day each.

Car hire gives you more freedom to follow these itineraries but each place is easily accessible by Catalunya's excellent public transport system, using train, bus, cable car or boat.

DON'T MISS

*** Montserrat: magnificent monastery in dramatic mountain scenery.
*** Cava Country: a chance to see how sparkling wine is made and to taste the results.
*** Port Aventura: a great day out for kids in Spain's biggest theme park.
*** Figueres: home of the eccentric Dalí Museum.
** Empúries: fascinating Roman remains.
** Sitges: flamboyant nightlife and beautiful beaches.

Opposite: *Fun-loving Sitges has its peaceful side, too.*

Excursions

SITGES

South of Barcelona, the coast stretches away in a series of long, sweeping beaches which have given the area its name, **Costa Daurada**, or golden coast. Relatively undeveloped, the area attracts mainly Spanish visitors – with one big exception, the resort of **Sitges**.

Nobody could pretend Sitges was quiet. The town initially developed as a holiday resort for rich city residents, many of whom still have a second home on the beach. The resort blossomed in the 1960s, even under the austerity of the Franco regime, to become Spain's leading gay centre as well as a weekend hangout for young people from the city. **Carnival** in February is a riot with the gay community organizing its own agenda of unofficial events, including an exuberant **drag parade** on Mardi Gras.

By day, however, Sitges is a pleasant fishing village turned holiday resort with two big, sandy beaches right in the town. Further out, there are nudist beaches and even gay nudist beaches. The town has a couple of sights worth visiting, although life in Sitges for most involves commuting slowly between the attractive, open-air coffee bars and the beach.

Museums *

Overlooking the beaches is a little hill, topped by the parish church that the locals call La Punta and lined with some smart old mansions. One of these is a fairly eccentric museum, **Cau Ferrat**, former home of the artist Santiago Rusiñol (1861–1931). The interior has been left virtually as it was found, a jumble of Rusiñol's work and various purchases and gifts, including paintings by **El Greco** and **Picasso** as well as some of the artist's lesser known friends who used to congregate in Els Quatre Gats in Barcelona. Open 09:30–14:00, 16:00–18:00, Tuesday–Saturday, 09:30–14:00, Sunday.

Next door in the **Palau Maricel de Mar** is a small, mixed collection of Romanesque and Gothic paintings, an attractive collection of Spanish ceramics, and wall paintings by the artist Josep Maria Sert (1874–1945). One more museum in the old part of the town, the **Museu Romàntic** displays everyday items from the life of a wealthy family in the 18th and 19th centuries, including music boxes and puppets. Both museums open 09:30–14:00, 16:00–18:00, Tuesday–Saturday, 09:30–14:00, Sunday.

Sitges by night

Nightlife in Sitges is fast and furious, concentrated mainly in the town centre. The carrer 1er Maig is the heart of the action with one long line of discos, pubs, restaurants and cocktail bars. Some discos are exclusively gay but there's generally a happy atmosphere in Sitges and holiday-makers mix cheerfully with drag queens, partygoers and artists. Having said this, Sitges is probably not the best choice for the faint-hearted.

THE PICASSO TRAIL

Various Picassos are displayed in locations other than the Picasso Museum in Barcelona. In the Museu de Montserrat there are four drawings and two oils as well as a lithograph of the *sardana*. There are five small works in the Cau Ferrat Museum in Sitges and some ceramic work at the Museu Ceràmica in Pedralbes. The Centre Picasso d'Horta at Horta de Sant Joan has a collection of reproductions of the work Picasso did when he stayed in the area and a library and archive dedicated to the artist. Finally, the Quatre Gats bar in the city displays some reproductions, printed work and journals.

Below: *Bronzed bodies pack the beach at Sitges.*

WINE COUNTRY
Sant Sadurní ★★★

A tour of Barcelona province's wine growing areas can be made using public transport from the city or by hiring a car. As you head south, industrial suburbs give way to rolling vineyards, the fruit of which produces 100 million bottles a year of *cava*, the Spanish version of *methode champenoise*.

Just half an hour from Barcelona by train, the town of Sant Sadurní has been the heart of the cava-producing region for over 100 years. The wine industry grew hand in hand with Catalan cork production (from the cork oaks in the forests) and exported cava to the rest of Europe when the French vineyards were struck by the Philoxera plague at the end of the 19th century.

The first wine grower to try the Champagne method here was **Josep Raventós i Domènech**, copying the techniques of Dom Perignon in 1872. His family still produces one of the best labels today, **Codorníu**, and tours of the cellar can be arranged. The Codorníu building is of particular interest – designed by Puig i Cadafalch, its elegant, ivy-draped appearance blends in well with the rolling vineyards that surround the town.

The other big producer is **Freixenet**, whose cellars are located opposite the train station. Tours and tastings can be arranged here as well.

Below: *The area around Sant Sadurní is known for its champagne-like wines.*

Vilafranca del Penedès

A large, attractive town, Vilafranca is the capital of the region's wine industry and has been a bustling market centre since the 11th century. Vilafranca was actually founded to encourage settlers to inhabit land left vacant by the expelled Moors. Many of the medieval mansions remain. The town is easily accessible from Barcelona by train or a short drive, making this an ideal half day trip. Should you be visiting at the end of August, be sure to attend the Festa Major when the streets are packed with processions, dances and *castellers* – somewhat drunken attempts to build human towers.

The wines from this area are almost all white, produced from three types of grape: **Macabeu**, **Xarel.lo** and **Parellada**. Wine *bodegas* (cellars) are dotted all over the town and most of them arrange tours and tastings. Look out for the *porrones*, flasks with long, pointed spouts from which the wine is poured with a flourish into the mouth, a sure way to get drunk quicker! One of the biggest producers here is **Torres**, a flagship producer for the whole of Spain, whose dry, fruity Vina Sol is exported all over the world. Good wines to try are Gran Vina Sol, the flowery Esmeralda, Gran Coronas and Los Torres Merlot.

The **Wine Museum** is worth a visit. Located in a 12th-century palace that was once home of the Kings of Aragón, it tells the story of wine production and drinking from Roman times up to the 15th century. On the museum's upper floor, there are relics from the city's history as well as ceramics, coins and work by 19th-century Catalan painters. Open 10:00–14:00, 16:00–19:00, Tuesday–Sunday.

Above: *Legend says the Pont del Diable was built by Hannibal.*

DEVIL'S BRIDGE

At the town of Martorell, outside the city is a highly unusual bridge, the Pont del Diable, which crosses the River Llobregat. Popular legend says that the bridge was built by Hannibal in 21BC with its central triumphal arch in memory of his father Hamilcar Barca, allegedly the founder of Barcelona. The less romantic reality is that the Romans built the bridge, which was extended in the Middle Ages and is in a remarkable state of repair today.

Right: *Stunning Roman remains can be found in the city of Tarragona.*

ONWARDS TO TARRAGONA

Another hour or so further along the coast on the highway is the beautiful town of Tarragona, former capital of the Roman province and a paradise for keen hunters of Roman remains. Visit the old town on foot by following the Passeig Arqueològic, a pathway between the city's Roman walls and the much newer outer fortifications, built in 1707. Every so often there's a *mirador* (lookout point) either over the plains or the sea, and historic paraphernalia is displayed along the route including Roman columns and 1000-year-old cannons.

Within the walls of the medieval old town is the cathedral, a mixture of Gothic and Romanesque styles, and two fascinating museums covering the city's history and archaeological treasures. Beneath the town, on the grassy slopes leading down to the sea is a magnificent Roman amphitheatre, while along the Rambla Valla are the remains of the Roman circus, Circ Romà, where chariot racing took place. Open 10:00–20:00, April–September, Tuesday–Saturday, 10:00–15:00, Sunday, 10:00–17:30, Tuesday–Saturday during winter.

The most spectacular remains, however, are at the Museu i Necropolis Paleocristians. Excavations of this vast burial site have revealed pagan and Christian tombs dating back to the 3rd century AD, the riches of which are displayed in the museum. Look for urns, tombs, sarcophagi and Visigothic sculpture. Open 10:00–13:00 and 16:30–20:00, Tuesday–Saturday, 10:00–14:00, Sunday.

THE SACRIFICIAL STONE

Near the inland town of Savassona is the eerie Pedra dels Sacrifis, a huge sandstone block with a horizontal groove and a series of cavities on one side. The stone is believed to have been used for ritual sacrifices and has given rise to all sorts of legends of witchcraft. The setting undoubtedly has some ancient religious purpose; excavations have uncovered an Iberian village dating to the 3rd century BC and earlier evidence of settlement in the first Iron Age. Neolithic graves have also been found nearby and to the east, flat stones have been engraved with human figures, crosses and circles.

PORT AVENTURA

Spain's biggest and most expensive adventure theme park (10:00–20:00, March to November; open until 24:00 in late June, July and August) opened on the Costa Daurada in 1995. The park is easily accessible from Barcelona by road and rail and was quick to become a major attraction for Catalunya.

Port Aventura may not be particularly Spanish, but it makes a great day out for the family. There are plenty of facilities and food stalls in addition to 30 bars and restaurants. Most of the products for sale are made by the artisans in the craft centres and range from bark paintings to coconut carvings and glass engravings. Visitors can have their purchases sent to the gate for collection when they leave the park.

Allow at least a day for a visit. The park is divided into five areas, a Mediterranean port, a Polynesian village, a Chinese fishing harbour and Imperial Palace, a recreation of Mayan Mexico and a Wild West frontier town. Visitors travel around the park by boat, steam train or on foot.

The **Mediterranean** section doubles as reception area and craft shops here sell leather goods and interesting ceramics. The Estació de Nord steam train takes passengers to the other areas.

PORT AVENTURA FACTS

- 170 permanent workers and 2500 seasonal staff.
- 70 choreographed street performances every day.
- 62 main shows a day ranging from Chinese acrobats to Country and Western.
- 46 full-time actors.
- 2.7 million people visited the park in its first year.
- The Dragon Khan ride is featured in the Guiness Book of Records with more loops than any other roller coaster in the world.

Below: *The walls of Tarragona's cathedral display intricate stonework.*

LA MORENETA

The statue you see today is around 800 years old, a stunning example of Romanesque culture. No-one knows why the face and hands are black – it could be years of exposure to candle smoke, the varnish that was once applied to the wood, or a coating of silver that may once have covered the statue. One theory is that the black colour of this statue is deliberate; when an older version was replaced, the monks wanted the new one to look the same.

Dancers in grass skirts and exotic bird displays add a South Pacific feel to the string of man-made islands that makes up the **Polynesian** section. The **Tutuki Splash** is the most popular ride here, hoisting 'boats' up into the heart of a volcano only to send them plummeting into the lagoon below, drenching both passengers and onlookers.

The **Chinese** area contains the park's most famous ride, **Dragon Khan**, a record-breaking roller coaster painted with images of a fiery dragon that rattles around at speeds of up to 110kph (68mph) and loops the loop eight times. The ride is supposed to reconstruct the legend of a Chinese prince who was turned into a dragon after trying to usurp the emperor but after the first loop, most people lose interest in mythology.

In the **Mexican** section, there's a reconstruction of the ancient pyramid of Chichen Itza surrounded by steamy jungles, wafting scents of Mexican food and pulsating Mariachi rhythms. The best ride here is **El Diablo**, another plummet from on high, this time in the guise of a runaway train in a Mexican silver mine.

A dusty saloon bar and a western stunt show in the **Wild West** form quite a contrast to Mexico. Rides include the **Grand Canyon Rapids**, 550m (1805ft) of man-made turbulent water, and the **Silver River Flume**, a gentle drift on log-shaped boats.

Right: *Port Aventura makes a great day out for children and adults alike.*
Opposite: *Montserrat perches high on the mountainside, carved into sheer rock.*

MONTSERRAT

Spain's most important pilgrimage after Santiago de Compostela, the jagged mountain of Montserrat, an hour by the FF.CC train from the city, is shrouded in legend and mystery. The mountain itself is incredibly beautiful, rising up from the plain like a row of jagged teeth. The monastery is cut precariously into the rock, sheltered by a row of wind and rain-blasted limestone towers.

Many areas of outstanding natural beauty inevitably inspire legend and Montserrat is no exception. The mountain has a magical quality any-way, particularly at sunrise as its cloak of mist begins to lift. Originally, 1000 years ago, hermits lived in huts and caves on the mountain because it was supposed to be a holy place, once visited by St Peter who left an icon of the Virgin Mary in a cave.

There is indeed a statue, **La Moreneta**, an unusual carving with a black face and hands. Legend has it that the icon went missing during the Moorish invasion of the 8th century, only to reappear in the late 9th century. A shrine was built around the statue, but in the 12th century it was replaced by a Romanesque building, part of which still stands today. The Virgin of Montserrat became the patron saint of Catalunya and her fame spread far and wide. It is from this shrine, for example, that the Caribbean Island of Montserrat takes its name.

The monastery has suffered badly over the last 200 years. In 1811, when Napoleon's forces invaded Catalunya, the hermits were driven away or killed and the monastery, filled at the time with amazing wealth, was sacked and partly destroyed. What is left of the building today is a mixture of late 16th-century Gothic and Modern (19th-century in style).

MONTSERRAT FLORA AND FAUNA

Thick woods of holm oaks grow in the mountain's nar-row gullies along with aleppo pine, maples, strawberry and hazelnut trees. Higher up, rosemary, thyme, juniper and heather fill the air with their scents. Animal life these days is restricted to stone martens, bats, geckos and the odd snake, although wolves and wild deer inhabited the slopes until recently. Lower down, squirrels, genets and wild boar are occasionally seen in the woods.

Above: *Hundreds of flickering candles light the atmospheric grotto at Montserrat.*

Montserrat is important to Catalans because it is a symbol of the region's revival. When the abbey was restored in the mid 19th century it marked the beginning of Catalunya's cultural renaissance and architects of the time, particularly Gaudí, were inspired in their work by the bizarre rock formations, now immortalized in the nativity façade of the Temple of the Sagrada Família.

During the 20th century the monastery's population dwindled, as 25 monks were killed in the civil war and it is only since 1939 that their numbers have revived. There are now some 80 monks living at Montserrat as well as 50 students at the world-famous choir school.

Montserrat today is one of Catalunya's most important tourist attractions, for its spectacular mountain scenery as much as for its religious significance. In addition to thousands of tourists and pilgrims, the trip here is made by hundreds of newlyweds.

The Basilica ★★★

The visit begins with a breathtaking ascent of the mountain face by cable car to just below the monastery. Alternatively, drive up the zigzagging mountain road. Outside the monastery, a small city has sprung up to accommodate the thousands of tourists – there is a restaurant, several souvenir shops, an information centre and even a bakery. In the monastery, only the basilica, dating from the late 16th century, is open to the public. Long queues form to kiss the famous statue, enthroned at one end.

The Escolania ★★

Three times a day, Montserrat's world-famous boys' choir sings hauntingly beautiful hymns and prayers. They perform all year round. The choir is supposedly the oldest in Europe, its earliest reference dating back to the 11th century, though there is actual documented evidence of choirboys at Montserrat in 1307. Fifty boys currently live and study in the monastery, which is known throughout Europe as a recruiting round for talented musicians.

Santa Cova ★★

There are several other things to see at Montserrat and it is worth allowing time for hiking the mountain's wooded trails to the various hermitages.

A cable car descends from just below the monastery to Santa Cova, the holy grotto, where the original Virgin icon is said to have been left by St Peter. Open 10:00–19:00 every 15 minutes daily.

A tiny chapel was built here in the 17th century, containing a replica of the statue. Alternatively, a path twists down through the woods, taking about 45 minutes, with breathtaking views of the Llobregat River Valley below.

A second cable car heads up the mountain from the monastery to Sant Joan, where a short trail leads to a mountain restaurant. An hour's walk across the ridge leads almost to the summit, Sant Jeroni, at 1236m (4055ft). Serious hikers may want to spend a night on the mountain at either of the two tiny refuges. This is possible if one obtains permission from the Catalan Excursion Society in Barcelona.

Museu de Montserrat ★

The Monastery Museum has two sections. The old part includes architectural remains from the hermitages on the mountain and some excellent paintings with work by El Greco and Caravaggio, while the new area features mainly 19th-century Catalan art. Open 10:30–14:00 in the old part, 15:00–18:00 in the new part.

CARDONA

Further inland from Montserrat is a spectacular Romanesque castle, over-looking the sleepy town of Cardona from an imposing hilltop position. The castle's 11th-century chapel now contains the tombs of the Dukes of Cardona, who lived in the castle. Part of the castle, which is supposed to be haunted, has now been converted into a *parador*, a government-run hotel and restaurant, providing luxurious accommodation and spectacular Catalan cuisine. On the way to the castle, look out for the Salina, a vast salt mountain left over from the town's salt mining days.

Below: *The weird rock formations at Montserrat were a source of inspiration to Gaudí.*

HEALTH SPAS

Need to take the cure?
Catalunya has several health
spas including one within
driving distance of Barcelona.
Balneari Titus is located
at Arenys de Mar, once
frequented by the Romans,
in a beautiful setting overlooking the sea and can be
visited for a day of hydro-
therapy, mud wraps, algae
baths, acupuncture and
lymph drainage, followed
by a gentle sunbathe on
the terrace. The resort can
be reached by motorway
from Barcelona or by
RENFE rail services.

COLONIA GÜELL

A short drive or train journey from Barcelona, the Colònia
Güell is another extraordinary work by Gaudí. At the end
of the 19th century Gaudí's patron, the industrialist
Eusebio Güell, constructed a velvet factory and a workers'
cooperative of 100 houses and a school next to a farm on
some family land outside Barcelona. The *modernista* building of the factory itself was designed by Gaudí's colleague
Francesc Berenguer while Gaudí worked on the colony's
church, laying the foundation stone in 1899.

Gaudí used a new technique to calculate the shape of
the church, hanging numerous lead weights in small bags
from strings to determine the stresses on the inverted
shape of the structure. A copy of the model is displayed in
the museum under the Sagrada Família and is worth a
moment's study for anyone interested in structure. The
result of this experiment was that the crypt alone was supposed to carry the weight of the chapel above, supported
only by four slender, slanted columns of basalt rock.

Only the crypt, one of Gaudí's more modest but most
impressive works, was finished. Resembling a cave, the
walls are crooked and the brickwork irregular – Gaudí's
way of expressing the asymmetry of nature. The crypt
is open every day but permission needs to be obtained
from the rectory.

Below: *The rocky coves
and clear water of Lloret
de Mar attract crowds
of sunworshippers.*

COSTA BRAVA

Around 60km (37 miles) north of Barcelona the industrial suburbs have faded away and the coastline starts to get interesting as the Costa Brava begins, its wooded coves, sharp cliffs, hidden bays and deep blue sea stretching all the way north to the French border.

In the 1960s this was one of the first areas of the Spanish coast to be developed for mass tourism, the price of which is paid today in resorts like **Lloret de Mar** and **Tossa de Mar**, concrete jungles of tower blocks and international cuisine. There are still plenty of outstandingly beautiful, unspoilt areas, however, which make this coast so rewarding to explore independently.

Above: *Tossa de Mar epitomizes the more scenic aspects of the coast.*

Lloret de Mar *

Big, bold and brash, Lloret towers over its coves and beaches, where thousands of pale north Europeans toast themselves under the sun by day and party at night. The fragments of an old town remain around the Plaça de l'Església but hedonism rather than history is the essential flavour of Lloret. This is a fun place to spend a few undemanding days and nights and can make a base from which to explore the region, although accommodation is hard to come by in July and August if you don't book on to a package tour.

Tossa de Mar **

A complete contrast, Tossa de Mar, 12km (7½ miles) to the north, is a walled tangle of streets and 12th-century buildings perched on a rocky headland. The town was originally Roman although most of what remains is 12th- to 14th-century and the old town, the **Vila Vella,** is a delightful maze of whitewashed buildings, window

Above: *Fishing is still a part of daily life in Tossa de Mar.*

boxes flaming with geraniums in summer. Of course, Tossa also sustains a thriving holiday market and has its share of high-rise buildings away from the old town, yet it remains worth a visit for its cultural interest. The small museum, **Museu de la Vila Vella**, has some Chagall paintings on display – the artist was fond of painting the landscapes of the 'wild coast'. In the evenings, the old town comes alive with people wandering through the twisting alleys and stopping to eat at the many outdoor restaurants. Open 10:00–13:00 and 15:00–18:00, Monday–Saturday, 10:00–13:00, Sunday.

Sant Feliu de Guixols **

From Tossa de Mar, the coast road becomes a series of perilous hairpin bends, twisting and turning with constant flashes of deep blue sea. Sant Feliu is actually over 1000 years old, having developed around a Benedictine monastery whose remains still stand on the Plaça Monestir; Visigothic and Roman walls can still be seen under the Torre de Fum. In the 19th century the town grew around its cork and boat-building industries and so has an authentic feel about it, particularly in the old part, despite the inevitable bars and cafés that have sprung up. There are three lovely beaches, all within easy reach of the town centre.

ROMANYA DE LA SELVA

Inland from Sant Feliu is one of the best preserved megalithic tombs (underground burial chambers) in Catalunya, Cova d'en Daina. Discovered at the end of the 19th century, the tomb was declared a national monument in 1931 and was properly excavated in the 1960s. All that remains is a circle of granite stones surrounding what would have been the burial mound, with a rectangular chamber covered by a roof of three slabs and accessed by a passage at the centre. To reach the site, follow the path to the left 1.5km (0.9 miles) along the road from the village towards Sant Antoni de Calonge.

Palamós *

Originally founded in 1277, Palamós is a busy fishing town set around a picturesque harbour. The fishing industry is still active and there are fish auctions every afternoon. There's a good beach in the town but otherwise, very little of historic or cultural interest.

Palafrugell **

Nestling in a beautiful valley 4km (2½ miles) inland from the rocky coastline, this 16th-century market town has virtually escaped the ravages of development. The old section is clustered around the main square, ringed with outdoor cafés where locals sit and gossip or read the paper. Three beautiful beaches are a short drive or a long walk away, past golden wheat fields to a coastline thick with bottle-green pines that contrast with tiny turquoise coves. **Calella** is the largest resort, connected to its neighbour **Llafranc** by a winding coastal path, while **Tamariu** is more isolated and quieter. All three are fairly upmarket, with white, low-rise villas clinging to the cliff face and smart yachts bobbing in their respective harbours.

Pa amb Tomàquet

Pa amb tomàquet is a typical taste of Catalunya and you'll see people eating it everywhere – at breakfast, as a snack or as a hors d'oeuvre. Consisting of crusty bread rubbed with salt, olive oil and fresh plum tomatoes, the dish varies from disappointingly soggy to delicious. If you're self-catering or making a picnic, make your own with good, dense bread that will absorb the liquids and toast it slightly first to keep the bread crunchy.

Empúries ***

Still just about accessible from Barcelona as a day trip, Empúries, 45 minutes to the north of Palafrugell, is best known for its interesting Roman remains. The town was founded by the Greeks in 550BC as a trading post, before the Romans moved in and developed an amphitheatre, luxurious villas and a marketplace. The Romans were later forced out and Empúries was taken over by the Visigoths, who left their own legacy of several basilicas. The 40ha (99 acre) site is still being excavated and is a fascinating place to wander around.

Below: *Tiny, hidden coves line the coastline of the Costa Brava.*

Around the ancient port are the remains of the **Greek** colony, including the foundations of various temples and a replica of a 3rd-century-BC statue of the god Asklepios. Above the Greek town are the cisterns where the Romans stored their water which was then piped around the villas. A few foundations and mosaics remain, as well as the ruined **Visigothic** churches.

Further inland, the continuing excavations of the **Roman** town are located, including two large villas with stunning mosaic designs and gardens. The amphitheatre and forum can also be seen, as well as the perimeter walls. For a clear explanation of the site, visit the museum by the cisterns. Some of the more valuable finds, however, are housed in the archaeological museum on Montjuïc in Barcelona. It is a good idea to visit the museum before Empúries for valuable background information. Open 10:00–14:00 and 15:00–20:00, Tuesday–Sunday.

Sant Marti ★

Just along the beach from Empúries is the small but bustling resort of Sant Marti, a pretty, walled village overlooking the vast stretch of the Golfo de Roses, a semicircular bay leading north to the last big holiday development before the French border, Roses; part of the bay's hinterland is a remote, unspoilt national park.

Below: *Extensive Roman ruins at Empúries.*
Opposite: *The Dalí Museum in Figueres is the second most visited in Spain.*

Figueres ★★★

The main reason to visit the otherwise uninspiring inland provincial town of Figueres, at the northern end of the Costa Brava, is to see the amazing **Dalí Museum**, astonishingly the most visited museum in Spain after the Prado in Madrid – more popular, even, than the Picasso Museum in Barcelona.

Dalí opened the museum in 1974, converting the former municipal theatre, a 19th-century building that had burned down in the civil war and fallen into a state of decay. The museum today is quite a sight; red, fortress-like walls topped with giant eggs and a huge, sparkling dome, the eerie Torre Galatea, where the artist spent his dying years, attached to it on one side. Inside, a sculpture garden has replaced the old theatre stalls and a series of rooms contains increasingly bizarre works, including Rainy Taxi, whereby water sprays into a Cadillac when coins are inserted. Well known works on the ground floor include *Soft Self Portrait with a Slice of Grilled Bacon* and *Portrait of Picasso*. Where the stage once was is a backdrop for a ballet, *Labyrinth*, and a portrait of Dalí's wife, Gala. On the first floor, visit the **Wind Palace Room** where there's a large fresco of two figures pouring gold coins through drawers onto the plain below.

Dalí claimed that his work was inspired by dreams and the theories of Sigmund Freud but his erotic paintings and peculiar landscapes were constantly challenged by other members of the surrealist school. True Dalí fans can go on from the museum to the artist's former home in Port Lligat near Girona, where guided tours are arranged by appointment for a nominal fee.

DALI

Salvador Dalí Domènech was born in Figueres in 1904 and had his first exhibition here aged 14. Dali was a controversial figure, rebelling against the artistic trends of his time, publishing questionable material and running away to Paris with Gala, the wife of his friend Paul Eluard. He wrote two books and several screenplays as well as painting prolifically, and lived the high life on the then fashionable Costa Brava. He created his museum in 1974 and returned to Figueres in the 1980s (after being severely burned by a fire), where he lived as a recluse in the Torre Galatea next to the museum until his death in 1989.

Above: *Colourful old houses are crammed along the riverbank in Girona.*

GIRONA

Quite unlike any other city in Catalunya, Girona bears strong traces of the Moors who inhabited it for 200 years and of the once-thriving Jewish community that lived here for six centuries. The walled city was originally built by the Romans and has been fought over countless times for its strategically important position on a hilltop on the Riu Ter.

What remains today is an astonishingly beautiful and well preserved city, a delight to wander around for a day. The old city is still walled on one side and bordered on the other by the river, and is best explored on foot for the occasional glimpse into a leafy courtyard or foray up a narrow alley.

Highlights of Girona are the **Cathedral**, mostly Gothic but partly dating back to the 11th century, with a lovely Romanesque cloister. The vault, at 22m (72ft), is the largest in the world, topped by brilliant, stained glass. Just opposite are the **Banys Arabs**, well preserved Arab baths consisting of three rooms based on the Roman concept of underfloor heating. There are two excellent museums to visit, the **Museu d'Art** (open 10:00–19:00, Tuesday–Saturday, 10:00–14:00, Sunday) and the **Museu Arqueològic** (open 10:00–13:00 and 16:30–19:00, Tuesday–Saturday, 10:00–13:00, Sunday), both telling the history of the city through Roman relics and stones bearing Jewish inscriptions.

The **Call**, or Jewish quarter, is one of the best preserved in Europe, dating back to the 9th century. The area is a city within itself where 300 Jews lived peacefully until their persecution began at the end of the 14th century. The Jews spent their last 100 years in Spain living in a ghetto and a wander through the dark streets gives a feeling of the claustrophobia they must have suffered.

INSIDE GIRONA

Try to spend a night in Girona, a city which deserves more than a day trip. Like Barcelona, the city has a Rambla where everybody takes their evening *passeig*. Throughout July there are live bands here on Wednesdays at 10:00 and *sardanas* are danced on Fridays throughout the summer. Nightlife revolves around the new part of the city across the river from the old town where there are rows of excellent bars alongside the majestic Parc de la Devesa. In winter, the bars around Plaça Ferran el Catòlic are more popular. For a quieter scene, there are plenty of places to eat and drink in the old quarter.

ANDORRA

The furthest organized tours from Barcelona make the 4½ hour journey north into the Pyrenees, to the tiny principality of Andorra. For many, the chief interest here is the duty-free shopping, yet the mountain scenery is stunning; high, craggy peaks, gushing torrents and thick pine forests.

Unfortunately, duty free status has turned much of Andorra's capital **Andorra la Vella** into a giant shopping mall and queues can form on busy days to get across the border from Spain. With time to spare, though, the surrounding mountains are fantastic walking country and the tourist office stocks good walking maps. In summer, fans of extreme sports flock to the **Noguera Pallaresa River** for white-knuckle, white water rafting and canoeing, while in winter the principality has several popular ski resorts, with the biggest selection of pistes at **Pal** and **Arinsal**. Not surprisingly, the resorts are packed at weekends and the atmosphere is lively; later in the season, around April, the sun beats down on lunchtime crowds basking outside the busy restaurants. The skiing is not particularly challenging but to city dwellers from Barcelona, the Pyrenees are the closest getaway for a weekend and the food and ambience make the trip worthwhile.

> **EATING IN ANDORRA**
>
> Not surprisingly, Andorra takes much of its cuisine from Catalunya and features several typically Catalan dishes like *butifarra*, a spiced pork sausage, and paella. Try *trinxat*, a local speciality made from green cabbage and mashed potato, more interesting than it sounds, and grilled trout from the mountain streams, a refreshing change from all the red meat. Festivals take place from the third weekend in July until mid-September, during which time assorted *coques* (cakes) are baked specially for the celebrations.

Overleaf: *Gaudí's Casa Batlló; the roof tiles are supposed to resemble a dragon's scales.*
Below: *As well as skiing, Andorra offers some stunning scenery.*

Barcelona at a Glance

BEST TIMES TO VISIT

Barcelona enjoys a typical **Mediterranean climate** of hot summers, mild winters and balmy spring and autumn seasons. The latter are the most conducive to wandering round the city, which is ideally suited to exploring on foot. **Winter**, however, has its advantages in that there are no queues to wait in. Some attractions will be closed in the winter months. This includes the Montjuïc cable cars and the amusement parks. Outdoor venues such as the **Poble Espanyol** and the **Olympic Marina** are also rather deserted and the coastal resorts are very quiet. **High summer** is usually too hot to pound the streets, although the evenings are pleasantly warm. Some restaurants shut down in August, when Spaniards take their annual holiday, and the coastal resorts, not surprisingly, are packed at this time.

GETTING THERE

Barcelona is accessible by road, rail, air and sea with domestic connections vastly improved since the Olympic Games in 1992.
The ultra-modern airport, **Aeroport del Prat**, is located southwest of the city, 25 minutes from the centre by taxi. A wide range of countries is also served from Madrid, with good internal connections to Barcelona.

Motorways (autopista) connect the city to the French border, one and a half hours away, and to the rest of Spain. Travelling around Catalunya by **road** is easy; Girona, Tarragona and Valencia are all accessible via the motorway. Other roads include autovia, dual carriageways and carretera estatal, all good main roads.
Sants-Estació is the city's main railway station. There are several types of trains: RENFE is the national rail company and trains vary from Pendular (the fastest inter-city services) to Talgo and Electrotren to Expreso and Rapido (ironically the slowest, regional services). English is spoken at the RENFE office at Sants.

GETTING AROUND

Barcelona has an excellent **Metro** system, easy to use, clean, punctual and relatively safe. The best value is a block of 10 tickets which gives considerable savings over 10 singles. Local women seem quite nervous on the Metro at night so tourists should follow their example: always sit with other people, guard your belongings and after about 21:00 or towards the end of the lines, take a taxi. Barcelona's 11,000 **taxis** are convenient and not particularly expensive. They can be hailed on the street or found on taxi ranks. A green light on the top means the taxi is free.

Drivers do not tend to speak English but all taxis are metered so communication is rarely a problem. There's an extra tax for travel with large pieces of luggage. Tips are appreciated but not expected. **Buses** also run all over the city and a special tourist bus operates in summer, the Bus Turístic or Bus 100. During the summer season, from mid-June to mid-October, the Bus Turístic runs on two circular routes, stopping (26 stops in all) at the main places of interest in the city. The ticket is valid all day and allows passengers to get on and off the bus for as many times and for as long as they want, as well as obtain major discounts on some visits. The ticket is purchased on board. Service starts and ends at Plaça Catalunya. In addition, there's an **antique tram** (Tramvia Blau) running from Tibidabo train stop to a funicular railway which travels to the top of the mountain. **Cable cars** operate from the top of Montjuïc to the harbour and on to Barceloneta, with sweeping views of the port. **Trains** leave Sants railway station for **Sitges** every half an hour. The Sitges station, behind the town, is about 20 minutes from the beach. Getting to **Montserrat** is easy. FF.CC trains (commuter trains – Ferrocarils de la Generalitat de Catalunya)

Barcelona at a Glance

depart from the Plaça d'Espanya for Manresa. Leave the train at the Montserrat Aeri stop and take the cable car, which runs every 15 minutes, to the monastery. One of the best ways to travel up the **Costa Brava**, just 60km (37½ miles) to the north, is by **boat**. Crucero boats depart from **Lloret de Mar**, the first big resort, calling at most major ports to the north. For a schedule, tel: (972) 36-4499.

WHERE TO STAY

Barcelona has a wide range of hotels from deluxe five star to basic *pensions* and *hostals*, which have fewer facilities. Hotels have a star rating from five-star Gran Luxe to one star. **Tourist offices** can usually provide accommodation information as can the **Gremi d'hotels de Barcelona**, via Laietana 47, (08003) Barcelona, tel: 93 301-4292.

Barri Gòtic and Seafront
LUXURY
Arts Barcelona, carrer Marina, 19-21 (08005), tel: 93 221-1000, fax: 93 221-1070. Luxury five-star hotel overlooking Olympic Marina and managed by the Ritz Carlton group. All rooms come with a CD player and have fabulous views of the city.
Colón, Av. Catedral, 7 (08002), tel: 93 301-1404, fax: 93 317-2915. Large,

traditional hotel in the heart of the Gothic quarter which faces the main façade of the cathedral.
Duques De Bergara, carrer Bergara, 11 (08002), tel: 93 301-5151, fax: 93 317-3442. Small, stylish establishment in the Gothic quarter.
Le Meridien Barcelona, La Rambla, 111 (08002), tel: 93 318-6200, fax: 93 301-7776. Modern chain hotel, air conditioned throughout.
Regente, Rambla de Catalunya, 76 (08008), tel: 93 487-5989, fax: 93 487-3227. Stylish *modernista*-style hotel well suited for nightlife.
Rívoli Ramblas, La Rambla, 128 (08002), tel: 93 302-6643, fax: 93 317-5053. Stark, modern design in central location.

MID-RANGE
España, carrer Sant Pau, 9 (08001), tel: 93 318-1758, fax: 93 317-1134. Attractive two-star hotel with quite an unusual restaurant design.
Gótico, carrer Jaume I, 14 (08002), tel: 93 315-2211, fax: 93 310-4081. Old-style hotel well located for sightseeing.
Hostal Layetana, Plaça Ramón Berenguer el Gran, 2 (08002), tel: 93 319-2012. Modest *hostal* overlooking the cathedral.
Oriente, La Rambla, 45 (08002), tel: 93 302-2558, fax: 93 412-3819. Reasonable rates and very central loca-

tion. Smart decor and attractive restaurant.
Regencia Colón, carrer Sagristans, 13–17 (08002), tel: 93 318-9858, fax: 93 317-2822. Modern and comfortable; all rooms come with a bath.
Rialto, carrer Ferran, 42 (08002), tel: 93 318-5212, fax: 93 318-5312. Mid-range establishment in the Gothic quarter.
Suizo, Plaça de l'Angel, 12 (08002), tel: 93 310-6108/315-0461, fax: 93 315-0461.

BUDGET
Las Flores, La Rambla, 79 (08002), tel: 93 317-1634. Simple *hostal* in central location.
Marina Folch, carrer Mar, 16 pral, (08003), tel: 93 310-3709/310-5327, fax: 93 310-1062. Clean but basic *hostal*.
Rey Don Jaime, carrer Jaume I, 11 (08002), tel: 93 310-6208, fax: 93 310-6208. Townhouse, all rooms with a bath, some with a balcony.

Eixample
LUXURY
Alexandra, carrer Mallorca, 251 (08008), tel: 93 487-0505, fax: 93 467-7166. Small, smart townhouse close to Passeig de Gràcia.
Claris, carrer Pau Claris, 150 (08009), tel: 93 487-6262, fax: 93 487-8736/215-7970. Grand five-star with all the facilities.

Barcelona at a Glance

Condes de Barcelona, Passeig de Gràcia, 73-75 (08008), tel: 93 488-2200, fax: 93 488-0614. Smart, modern hotel in prestigious location near the shops and *modernista* buildings.

Gran Hotel Catalonia, carrer Balmes, 142 (08008), tel: 93 415-9090, fax: 93 415-2209. Modern townhouse hotel near the shops.

Gran Hotel Havana, Gran Via de les Corts Catalanes, 647 (08010), tel: 93 412-1115, fax: 93 412-2611. Attractive building, 141 rooms and good facilities.

Majèstic, Passeig de Gràcia, 70 (08008), tel: 93 488-1717, fax: 93 488-1880. Large, busy hotel in central location.

Ritz, Gran Via de les Corts Catalanes, 668 (08010), tel: 93 318-5200, fax: 93 318-0148. Barcelona landmark, very grand and dignified in central location.

Mid-range

Balmes, carrer Mallorca, 216 (08008), tel: 93 451-1914, fax: 93 451-0049. Pretty townhouse hotel with small pool and garden.

Caledonian, Gran Via de les Corts Catalanes, 574 (08011), tel: 93 453-0200, fax: 93 451-7703. Small, centrally located townhouse. Ideal for shops.

Hostal Ciudad Condal, carrer Mallorca, 255 (08008), tel: 93 215-1040/487-0459. *Modernista* building near shops and bars.

Budget

Montserrat, Passeig de Gràcia, 114 (08008), tel: 93 217-2700. Good value hotel considering its prestigious location. Close to the Gaudí buildings.

Hostal-Residencia Oliva, Passeig de Gràcia, 32 (08007), tel: 93 488-0162 or 317-5087. Relaxed, airy *hostal* on top floor of large but characterful apartment block facing on to the Passeig de Gràcia.

Gràcia

Mid-range

There are not many hotels in Gràcia and these are the best available.

Rubens, Passeig Ntra. Sra. del Coll, 10 (08023), tel: 93 219-1204, fax: 93 219-1269. Large hotel with garden.

Via Augusta, Via Augusta, 63 (08006), tel: 93 217-9250, fax: 93 237-7714. Small, stylish hotel in peaceful location.

Montjuïc

Luxury

Barcelona Plaza Hotel, Plaça Espanya, 6-8 (08014), tel: 93 426-2600, fax: 93 426-0400. Large four-star hotel right on Plaça Espanya.

Fira Palace, Avinguda Rius i Taulet, 1-3 (08004), tel: 93 426-2223, fax: 93 425-5047. Large, modern hotel on Montjuïc, ideally located for trade fairs.

Budget

Hostal Béjar, carrer Béjar, 36-38, 1er. 3a. (08014), tel: 93 325-5953. Tiny hostel opposite the Parc Joan Miró. Basic facilities but it's clean and friendly.

Diagonal

Luxury

Princesa Sofía Inter-Continental Plaza Pio X11,4 tel: 93 330 7111, fax: 93 330 7621. Modern, luxury hotel on the Diagonal with excellent business facilities and service.

Barcelona Hilton, Avinguda Diagonal, 589-591 (08014), tel: 93 495-7777, fax: 93 405-2573. Big, modern five-star hotel with all the usual Hilton facilities.

Rey Juan Carlos I, Avinguda Diagonal, 661-671 (08028), tel: 93 364-4040, fax: 93 448-0607. Deluxe five-star hotel operated by Conrad Hotels, set in beautiful gardens with extensive sporting facilities.

Beyond Barcelona

Mid-range

There are not many hotels to choose from; these are the best available.

Abat Cisneros, Monestir de Montserrat, (08199), tel: 93 835-0251/835-0201, fax: 93 828-4006. Small hotel outside the monastery gates.

Hostal El Monestir, Monestir, s/n (the building has no number) (08199), tel: 93 835-0251. Basic hostel situated outside the monastery.

Barcelona at a Glance

Mas Pau, Avinyonet de Puiguentós, Carretera de Figueras 9, Besalú, tel: (972) 54-6154. Lovely old farmhouse near Figueras.

Barcelona has many restaurants. Some serve tapas at the bar as well as food at the table. Some tapas bars have dancing and live music. There are various specialist establishments; a *marisqueria* is a seafood restaurant, while *grill* usually means meat. A tapas bar may have in its title *tasques*, *cellers* or *cervecerias*, the latter serving beer rather than wine. A *bodega*, conversely, serves wine rather than beer, while a *xampanyería* specializes in *cava*. All the restaurants listed below specialize in local or regional Spanish cuisine.

Barri Gòtic
LUXURY
Set Portes, Passeig Isabel 11, tel: 93 319-2950. Grand Barcelona institution on the edge of La Ribera. Wonderful Catalan specialities.

MID-RANGE
Amaya, La Rambla 20-24 (Ciutat Vella), tel: 93 302-1037. Basque and seafood specialities.
Los Caracoles, Escudellers 14, tel: 93 302-3185. A Barcelona legend; Catalan specialities in rambling old building in the Barri Gòtic.

El Gran Café, Avinyó 9 (Ciutat Vella), tel: 93 318-7986. French/Catalan specialities with live piano music.
Hofmann's, Argenteria 74-78, tel: 93 319 5889 closed Saturday and Sunday. Great seafood and wicked desserts.
El Salon, c/Hostal d'en Sol 6-8, tel: 93 315-2159. Stylish bohemian feel with French/Catalan specialities.

BUDGET
Museo Picasso, Montcada 15 (Ciutat Vella), tel: 93 268-3021. Pretty bar/café in the courtyard of the Picasso Museum. Has the same opening hours as the museum.

Gràcia and Eixample
LUXURY
Botafumeiro, Gran de Gràcia 81 (Gràcia), tel: 93 218-4230. Expensive and prestigious seafood restaurant.

MID-RANGE
El Pescador, Mallorca 314 (Eixample), tel: 93 459-2564. Fish is their speciality.
Jean Luc Figueras, Sta. Teresa 10 (Gràcia), tel: 93 415-2877. Stylish setting and Catalan dishes.
Tragaluz, Passatje de la Concepcio, tel: 93 487-0196. Trendy bar downstairs, light-filled restaurant upstairs. Popular for business lunches.
La Cuina del Trope, Passeig de Gràcia 83 (Eixample). Home cooking in old Barcelona house.

La Gran Tasca, Balmes 129 bis (Example). Busy restaurant serving excellent tapas at the bar. Great atmosphere.
Casi Casi, c/Laforja 8, tel: 93 415-8194. Andalucian and Catalan cuisine.
El Raco d'en Freixa, Sant Elias 22, tel: 93 209 7559. Sublime, creative modern cuisine.

BUDGET
El Café de Internet, Gran Via 656 (Eixample), tel: 93 302-1154. Cyber café – computers to play with.
Drugstore David restaurante Pizzeria, Tuset 19-21. Famous, open all-night, tapas and pizza bar with shops in Eixample. Always busy. No telephone number available.

Seafront
LUXURY
Lungomare Ristorante, Marina 16-18 (Torre Mapfre), tel: 93 221-0428. Fashionable Italian in the Olympic Village.

MID-RANGE
El Rey de la Gamba, Porto Olimpic, tel: 93 221-0012. Fabulous seafood dishes for reasonable prices.
L'Emperador, Edif. Palau del Mar. Moll del Dipòsit, tel: 93 221-0220. Offering seafood specialities overlooking the marina.
Goyescas, Hotel Arts, Carrer de la Marina, 19 tel: 93 221 1000 Tapas to die for in the city's most stylish hotel.

Barcelona at a Glance

Llevataps, Plaça Pau Vila, s/n (Palau de Mar), tel: 93 221-2433. Seafood specialities overlooking the marina.

BUDGET
Can Majó, Almirall Aixada 23 tel: 93 221-5096. Fantastic, bargain seafood in old Barceloneta.

Greater Barcelona
LUXURY
Casa Ramón, Passeig St Joan Bosco 47 (Sarrià), tel: 93 205-7556. Grills and fondue a speciality.
El Asador de Aranda, Avinguda Tibidabo 31 (St Gervasil), tel: 93 417-0115. Catalan specialities in a spectacular old house.

Bars
Eating in one of the city's many bars is a great way to try tapas and save money. Bars range from very local to very lively; those around the Eixample district are mostly smart.

Barri Gòtic
Café de l'Òpera, La Rambla 74, tel: 93 302-4180. Touristy, art nouveau bar on the Rambla with expensive tapas. Always busy and safe for single women.
Café de Roma, Plaça Angel. Lively bar with invigorating liqueur coffees on the edge of the Barri Gòtic.

Els Quatre Gats, Montsió 3 bis (Ciutat Vella), tel: 93 302-4140. Charming bar situated in the old quarter once frequented by Picasso and friends.
Tèxtil Café, Museu Tèxtil I d' Indumentária, Montcada 12–14, tel: 93 268-2598. Pleasant café in the textile museum, opening hours same as museum.
Bar de Pi, Plaça Pi. Pretty bar located in a shady square off the Rambla, lively day and night.
Bar Ra, Plaça de la Garduña 7, tel: 93 301-4163. Tapas, tex-mex, and Thai food accompanied by music from jazz to rock.
El Velòdrome,c/Muntaner 213, tel: 93 430-5198. Trendy two-storey, art deco bar with leather sofas.

Eixample and Gràcia
Qu Qu, Passeig de Gràcia 24, tel: 93 317-4512. Great deli-style snacks and lively atmosphere.
Le Pedrera de Nit, c/Provença 261-5, Enjoy live music and drinks on the roof terrace of Gaudí's famous building. Open Saturday and Sunday during the summer only.
Seltz, Rosselló 154, tel: 93 453-6099 specialist vermouth bar with excellent tapas.
Tragaluz, Passatje de la Concepcio, tel: 93 487-0196 trendy bar with Japanese menu.

Seafront
Tardá Rock, Marina 16-18 Torre Mapfre (Port Olympic), tel: 93 221-3993. Barcelona's rock café, full of memorabilia. Tex-Mex food.

Greater Barcelona
Bar Tomás, Mayor de Sarrià 49, tel: 93 418-8855. Bar in Tibidabo area, attracting a lively crowd.

NIGHTCLUBS

Commonly known as *disco-tecas* (a 'club' usually refers to a sex show), Barcelona's nightspots are among the most sophisticated in Spain. Some are bars with dancing, while others are nightclubs only. Others have live entertainment. The *Guía del Ocio*, Barcelona's weekly listings guide, will have details of what's on in all the clubs.

Eixample and Gràcia
Blue Note, Aragó 221, tel: 93 454-6321. Live jazz performances.
Dry Martini, Aribau 162. Fashionable bar serving every possible permutation of a dry martini.
Garatge Club, Pallars 195. Live music and several dance floors.
Oliver & Hardy, Avinguda Diagonal, tel: 93 593-595, or 419-3181. Busy *discoteca*, open until 04:00.

Barcelona at a Glance

KGB, Carrer Alegre de Dalt 55, Gràcia, tel: 93 210-5906. Fashionable, warehouse-style club with spying theme.
Nick Havanna, Rosselló 208, tel: 93 215-6591. Trendy designer bar with cowhide-covered bar and huge video wall. Popular with 30-somethings after 01:00.
Universal, Marià Cubi 184, tel: 93 201-4658. Dancing and space for chilling out and conversation.
Otto Zutz, Lincoln 15, tel: 93 238-0722. Currently the trendiest of all, frequented by supermodels and young media types. Huge old warehouse conversion with dancing on three levels. Dress fashionably.

Montjuïc
Tablao de Carmen, Arcs 9 (Poble Espanyol), tel: 93 325-6895. Andalucían flamenco performances throughout summer; touristy but interesting and atmospheric.
Torres de Avilá, Marqués de Comillas, s/n, tel: 93 424-9309. Futuristic designer club in the Poble Espanyol.

Seafront
Maritimo Club, Moll de la Fusta 35 (no tel) Balearic house music, an outdoor dance floor and glamorous transvestites.
Tijuana Morning Café, Passeig Maritim 34, tel: 629 363337. Cavernous, Ibiza-inspired club on the beach. Open til 11:00.

THEATRES
Theatre performances are mainly in Catalan but should you wish to see a show, tickets are sold from the kiosk on the corner of carrer Aribau and the Gran Via. Alternatively, try the Centro de Localidades on Rambla Catalunya 2. There are four mainstream theatres in the city centre.

CASINOS
There are three casinos within driving distance of the city.

Barcelona
Gran Casino de Barcelona, Sant Pere de Ribles, tel: 93 893-3666.

Girona
Casino Castell de Peralada, Peralada, tel: (972) 53-8125.
Casino Lloret de Mar, Lloret de Mar, tel: (972) 36-6512.

SHOPPING
Barcelona is a shopper's dream, with everything from haute couture to typical ceramics on sale. For designer fashion, jewellery and furniture stores, the **Passeig de Gràcia** is the place to look, similar to London's Knightsbridge or New York's Fifth Avenue. Don't miss the fabulous **Vinçon** either, Barcelona's design emporium situated just next door to the Casa Milà.

The **Barri Gòtic** is best for browsing, with great art and antique shops as well as several *xocolateries* – high class confectioners. Along the **Rambla**, prices are inflated and quality lower, aimed mostly at tourists, although the flower stalls and bird market are fascinating for browsing. Remember to see **La Boquería** too, Barcelona's main market, open Monday–Saturday. Spain only has one famous department store chain, **El Corte Inglés**, which has two outlets in Barcelona, one on the Plaça de Catalunya and a second on the Diagonal. There are modern shopping malls along the Diagonal from the top of the Passeig de Gràcia to the Plaça Reina Maria Cristina, featuring international names such as **Marks & Spencer** and **Habitat**.
For fun style ideas to take home, visit the **Maremagnum Centre** opposite the Columbus statue where shops, tapas bars and restaurants are all under one roof overlooking the port. The best art posters are from the museums, and carrer Montcada, home of the Picasso Museum, has ceramics stores as well as endless poster shops. On Montjuïc, the Poble Espanyol sells typical souvenirs from all over Spain at rather inflated prices.

Barcelona at a Glance

TOURS AND EXCURSIONS

Typical coach tours in and around the city include half day and full day regular sightseeing excursions with several museum visits. Further afield, regular tours operate to Montserrat, *cava* cellars, Andorra and the Costa Brava. **Guided tours** in different languages are operated by:
Julià Tours,
Rda. Universitat 5, tel: 93 317-6454, fax: 93 318-5997.
Calesses (horse-drawn carriages), tel: 93 421-8804. Half an hour to an hour, round the major sites **Gaudí Tours**, tel: 93 450-0775. Or book on-line for specialist tours of Gaudí's heritage at: www.tours@barcelona.com

Harbour tours
Small sightseeing boats make regular excursions around the harbour.
Golondrinas, Portal de la Pau, s/n, tel: 93 442-3106. Departures: 11:00–18:00 every 30 minutes. Saturday, Sunday and public holidays, November–March. 11:00– 18:00, March–June and October. 11:00–20:30, July–September.

Torre de Collserola
Free transport from top of Tibidabo to the communications tower for spectacular views across the city and beyond. Open daily. Check times on tel: 93 211-7942.

Casa Milà, 'La Pedrera' Guided tours of Gaudí's famous apartment building including a visit to the roof. Visits must be booked in advance, tel: 93 487-3613 and 93 488-3592.

Museum tours
Fundació Antoni Tàpies, tel: 93 487-0315.
Museu Frederic Marés. Closed on Mondays, tel: 93 310-5800.
MNAC-Museu D'Art Modern, Parc de la Ciutadella, tel: 93 319-5728.
Museu Picasso. Closed on Monday, tel: 93 319-6310.
Fundació Joan Miró, tel: 93 329-1908.

Concert tours
Palau de la Música Catalana Closed in August. Visits by arrangement, tel: 93 268-1000.

Outside the city
To stay in the mountain refuges of Catalunya, including the two at Montserrat, get permission from the **Federació d'Entitats Excursionistes de Catalunya**, tel: 93 412-0777.

Montserrat information:
tel: 93 835-0251 ext. 586. Mass at Montserrat is sung at 11:00, 13:00 and 18:45.

USEFUL CONTACTS

Iberia Airlines of Spain Infoberia, tel: 93 412-5667 National bookings, tel: 93 412-7020 International bookings, tel: 93 412-4748
Airport, tel: 93 478-5000 www.iberia.com
RENFE (Spanish Railways), tel: 93 490-0202 www.renfe.es
Transmediterránea (ferry service), tel: 93 443-2532
FF.CC Generalitat (Autonomous Government Railways), tel: 93 205-1515
Tourist guides-interpreters, tel: 93 345-4221, 268-2422, 412-0674
Taxis, tel: 93 57-7755, 358-1111, 392-2222, 387-1000
Emergency Medical Service, tel: 061
Police, tel: 091
Police Assistance (Tourist Attention), tel: 93 301-9060 Lost property, tel: 93 318-5531
Directory Enquiries, tel: 1003
National Operator, tel: 1009

BARCELONA	J	F	M	A	M	J	J	A	S	O	N	D
AVERAGE TEMP. °F	50	49	53	53	64	71	74	77	69	60	53	51
AVERAGE TEMP. °C	10	10	11	11	18	22	23	25	20	16	11	11
HOURS OF SUN DAILY	6	5	6	6	7	9	9	9	6	5	4	3
RAINFALL ins.	2	2	2	3	1	1	1	0.5	1	4	2	2
RAINFALL mm	42	42	42	70	25	25	25	10	25	106	42	42
DAYS OF RAINFALL	5	6	6	9	5	4	4	2	5	9	6	6

Travel Tips

Tourist Information

The Spanish Tourist Board has offices in the United Kingdom (London); the USA (Chicago, Los Angeles, Miami and New York); Canada (Toronto); Australia (Sydney) and most European countries. Website: www.tourspain.es.

The Barcelona Town Hall website, packed with information, is: www.bcn.es.

Other useful sites include: www.barcelona.com and www.barcelona-on-line.es

Barcelona has its own, excellent tourist board with offices around the city: **Estació Barcelona Sants**, Plaça Països Catalans, s/n, station vestibule. Open 08:00–20:00, Monday–Friday, 08:00–14:00, Saturday, Sunday and public holidays. Open 08:00–20:00 daily in summer. Information about Barcelona only.

Tourist Information Office: Gran Via de Les Corts Catalanes 58, tel: 93 301 7443. Open 09:00–19:00, Monday–Friday, 09:00–14:00, Saturday. Closed on Sunday and public holidays.

Barcelona Airport, International Terminal, tel: 93 478 4704. Open 09:30–20:30, Monday–Saturday, 09:30–15:00, Sunday and public holidays. Tourist information about Barcelona, Catalonia and the rest of Spain. The tourist board also has a very active **Convention Bureau** for assistance with event planning and trade fairs.

Entry Requirements

All visitors need a **passport** or in certain cases, an **identity card**. Citizens of Andorra, Liechtenstein, Monaco, Switzerland and countries within the EC need only present an identity card, with the exception of Denmark and the UK, citizens of which need a passport. UK visitors must have a full 10 year passport as of 1995. US, Canadian and Japanese citizens require a passport but no visa. **Visas** are required by citizens of Australia and New Zealand. All visitors can stay up to 90 days, after which time a **residence permit** is required.

Customs

The maximum allowance for duty-free items brought into Spain is as follows: one litre of spirits or two of fortified wine; two litres of wine and 200 cigarettes. When the items are bought and duty paid for in the EC, the amounts are 10 litres of spirits, 90 litres of wine and 110 litres of beer, for private consumption only. There is little point bringing wine or beer into Spain, as they are cheap locally. You can no longer buy duty free goods if you are travelling within the EC. **Andorra** is entirely duty free and is a good place to buy cheap alcoholic drinks, cigarettes and perfume. Foreign currency, bankers drafts and travellers cheques can be imported and exported without being declared, but an upper limit applies – check before going. Spanish customs officials are generally polite and easy to negotiate with.

Health Requirements

No vaccinations are required to enter Spain and the only real health hazards are the occasional upset stomach and the sun, which is very strong during the summer months of June to September. EU citizens qualify for free medical treatment on presentation of the appropriate form (the **E111** for British citizens). Visitors from elsewhere should arrange their own travel and medical insurance.

Getting There

Barcelona is accessible by road, rail, air and sea.
By air: The modern airport, Aeroport del Prat, southwest of the city is 25 minutes away from the centre. There are good internal connections to Barcelona from Madrid. Charter flights from London and other European cities operate into Reus on the Costa Dorada to the south of the city, mainly to access the coastal resorts and the theme park Port Aventura. Barcelona is a day trip from Reus by car or train. Airlines: Iberia Airlines of Spain Flight information and reservations, tel: 93 412-7020 or 93 412-4748.
By road: The city is connected to the French border and to the rest of Spain via the motorway. If you bring your own car into the country and live outside the EC then a **Green Card** is necessary; third party insurance is compulsory. An **international driving licence** is also required. Driving in Spain is on the right. Hiring a car for a stay in Barcelona, however, is not necessary as the city's public transport system is so efficient. In order to hire a car, drivers must be over 21 with a year's driving experience. Don't leave anything in your car because

vehicle crime is a problem. Road conditions and travel information are available in Spanish on the **Teleruta** service, tel: 91 535 2222.
Speed limits are 120 kph (75 mph) on *autopistas*, 120, 100 or 80 according to signs on *autovias* (dual carriageways), 90 on country roads and 60 on urban roads. Stiff, on-the-spot speeding fines are not uncommon. The wearing of seatbelts is compulsory in the front and if fitted, in the back. **Motorcyclists** must wear safety helmets by law.
Buses: operate to Barcelona from Andorra, Bilbao, Costa Brava, Cordoba, Girona, Granada, Seville, Madrid, San Sebastian and numerous other Spanish and international cities. There are several different companies, each featuring different destinations. The best way to find out what's on offer is to call in at the **Estacio del Nord**, Avinguda Vilanova, tel: 93 265-6508. For buses between Barcelona and the Costa Brava, call Empresa Sarfa on tel: 93 318-9735.
By rail: Estacio-Sants is the city's main railway station, with trains linking Barcelona to the rest of Spain and Europe.
By boat: Ferries depart regularly from the Balearic Islands to Barcelona's Estacio Maritima at the end of the Rambla, and are operated by Trans-mediterranea, tel: 93 412-2524. Book in advance during the summer.

What to Pack

If you plan to take advantage of Barcelona's nightlife, **high fashion** is essential! This is a

---

USEFUL CATALAN PHRASES

Si, No, Val • Yes, No, OK
Si us plau, Gràcies (Merci in north Catalunya) • Please, Thank you
Hola, Adéu • Hello, Goodbye
Bona tarde/nit • Good afternoon/night
Com va? • How are you?
(No) ho entenc • I (don't) understand
Parleu anglés? • Do you speak English?
Em dic ... • My name is ...
Es massa car • It's too expensive
On és ...? • Where is ...?
Qué hi ha per menjar? • What is there to eat?

---

cosmopolitan city and you can never be too overdressed. Otherwise, **casual wear** is fine for sightseeing. Remember sunglasses and a hat for the summer and comfortable shoes for walking around the city, and **smart casual** for the evenings. Some restaurants will expect jacket and tie and people dress up for the opera. Show respect when entering the cathedral or churches, or visiting Montserrat – women should wear long skirts and cover their shoulders and men should not wear shorts. Some of the smarter hotels have swimming pools so bring swimming gear. Otherwise, Barcelona sells everything you could buy in any other big city.

Money Matters

In 2002 the euro replaced the peseta as the Spaniah **currency**. Notes are in denominations of 5, 10, 20,

50, 100, 200 and 500 euros, coins in values of 1 euro, 2 euros, 50 cents, 20 cents, 10 cents, 5 cents, 2 cents and 1 cent. There are **banks** and **exchange bureau** all over the city, some of which take overseas credit cards in their automatic tellers. Banking hours are 09:00–14:00, Monday–Friday and 09:00–13:00 on Saturdays, although they vary occasionally. Major **credit cards** are accepted although some country restaurants and small tapas bars may require cash. Holders of cards bearing the Visa, Mastercard, Cirrus and Plus signs can use Spanish automatic tellers, which have instructions in English. A fee is charged for this. **Travellers cheques** can be changed in banks and the Bureaux de Change which operate in the main resorts. Foreign banks include a Barclays, Chase Manhattan and NatWest on the Passeig de Gràcia; Bank of America on carrer Bori i Fontesta and Lloyds Bank on the Rambla de Catalunya and the Diagonal. The exchange bureau at the air-

port is open 07:45–10:45. Spanish **sales tax** (IVA) is currently 16% and is not always included in the price, so be aware of this when you buy a particular item. **Tipping** is optional; around 10% of the price of a meal is acceptable. Petrol pump attendants and taxi drivers also expect a small tip.

Accommodation

Hotels are rated with a star system with five stars being the highest. 'Gran Luxe' signifies a particularly luxurious hotel. **Apartment hotels** follow the same grades, the only difference being that they have cooking facilities in the rooms. **Hostals** and **pensions**, more basic establishments, are graded from one to three stars. **Camp sites** are rated luxury, first, second and third class and are plentiful. Each region, however, is responsible for its own classification, so accommodation gradings will vary. Most hotels belong to the group known as the **Barcelona Hotel**

Association; tel: 93 301-6240 for a hotel guide. Barcelona's **budget** accommodation tends to be around the **Rambla** and in the **Barri Gòtic**. The right hand side of the Rambla, towards the port, is the safest area. Hostals around the **Plaça de Catalunya** are more expensive but the area is quieter and less threatening at night. The hotels around **Passeig de Gràcia** tend to be the city's most expensive, but are favoured by many business travellers.

Paradors are government-run hotels, usually in historical buildings or areas of outstanding natural beauty. Contact **Paradores de Turismo**, carrer Requena 3, 28013 Madrid, tel: 91 559 0069, fax: 91 559 3233, www.parador.es **Estancias de España**, a private association of hotels and restaurants in historic buildings, produces a brochure detailing its 44 members, 15 of which are in Andalucía. Estancias de España, carrer Menendez Pidal, 31, bajo izqd. 28036 Madrid, tel: 91 345-4141, fax: 91 345-5174.

Eating Out

Barcelona has an enormous range of restaurants serving all kinds of **international cuisine** as well as **regional Spanish** and **Catalan dishes**. Tapas bars, tascas, bodegas, cervecerias and tabernas are all types of bar serving food. A tapas bar and tasca serve wine, beer, spirits and snacks, usually displayed at the bar. Many visitors, particularly those on

CONVERSION CHART		
FROM	**TO**	**MULTIPLY BY**
Millimetres	Inches	0.0394
Metres	Yards	1.0936
Metres	Feet	3.281
Kilometres	Miles	0.6214
Kilometres square	Square miles	0.386
Hectares	Acres	2.471
Litres	Pints	1.760
Kilograms	Pounds	2.205
Tonnes	Tons	0.984
To convert Celsius to Fahrenheit: x 9 ÷ 5 + 32		

a budget, happily substitute several dishes of tapas for an evening meal. A *bodega* specialises in wine, while a *cerveceria* serves beer. *Taberna* is a generic term for a bar or tavern. A *comedor* is a simple dining room, usually attached to a bar and a *venta* is a similar set-up in the countryside, usually with a small shop as well. A *marisqueria* specializes in seafood and an *asado* in barbecued food. In any restaurant, the *menu del dia* – the set menu – represents good value, usually including three courses and wine. Catalan restaurants are the most common and some of the more expensive blend French cuisine with local fish and meat specialities. For fast food, Barcelona has everything from Pizza Hut to Burger King, while ethnic specialities include German, Indian, Chinese, Middle Eastern and Mexican restaurants.

Transport

Barcelona has an excellent **Metro** system, easy to use, clean, regular and relatively safe. The best value is a block of 10 tickets which gives considerable savings over 10 singles. Local women do seem quite nervous on the Metro at night, though, so tourists should follow their example and always sit with other people. Guard your belongings and after about 21:00 or towards the end of the lines, take a taxi instead. Barcelona's 11,000 **taxis** are convenient and not particularly expensive.

They can be hailed on the street or found on taxi ranks. Drivers do not tend to speak English but all taxis are metered so communication is rarely a problem. There's an extra tax for travel with large pieces of luggage. In addition, there's an **antique tram** (Tramvia Bleu), and **cable cars** operate from the top of Montjuïc to the harbour and on to Barceloneta. A second, underground funicular connects the Paral.lel metro station to Montjuïc, emerging within walking distance of the Joan Miró foundation and the amusement park.

Business Hours: Shops and businesses generally open from 09:00 or 10:00 to 13:30 or 14:00 and close for a siesta. They reopen 16:00–20:00. Some businesses start much earlier, around 08:00 and work straight through to 15:00 with no siesta. Hours also change in the summer. Big department stores now stay open all day but most supermarkets close for lunch. In the resorts, the souvenir shops are open as late as 22:00 in summer.
Lunch tends to be served from about 13:00 to 16:00, with dinner from 20:00 (sometimes earlier for the benefit of the tourists) to 24:00. Bars and clubs stay open late on the coast – sometimes until 04:00.

Time Difference

Spain is on GMT+1 hour in winter and on GMT+2 hours from the last Sunday in March to the last Sunday in October in summer.

Communications

The international dialling code for Spain is +34 9. Each province has its own dialling prefix. The number for Barcelona is +34 93 when dialling from overseas or 93 when dialling from within Spain or Barcelona itself.Full instructions on the use of public telephones are shown in English in the kiosk. Cheap rates are between 22:00 and 08:00. To call overseas, dial 007 and wait for the tone to change before dialling the country code and the number. **Telephone cards** can be bought from Telefónica offices or tobacconists. Mobile phones operate on 1800 and 900 MHZ frequencies, with comprehensive coverage. The main, very grand **post office** (Correos) is at the end of the Passeig de Colom on Placa d'Antoni Lopez. Open 08:30–22:00, Monday – Saturday and 10:00–12:00, Sunday. There's a poste restante service here. Stamps can be purchased from tobacconists and hotel receptions.

Electricity

The power system is 220 or 225 volts AC. Older buildings occasionally have 110 or 125 volts AC and should be treated with extreme caution. Two pin plugs are used. Americans will need a transformer, British visitors an adaptor.

Weights and Measures

Spain uses the metric system.

Health Precautions

An excess of sun and sangría are the worst health problems encountered by most people. Use a high factor sun protection cream, wear a hat and take special care during the height of summer. Drink bottled water if you get a stomach upset. A mosquito repellant is also a good idea.

Health Services

Spanish pharmacists are highly trained and can dispense medicines often only available on prescription.

Opening hours are 09:00–13:30 and 17:00–20:30 (with the occasional half-hour variation). Every area has a duty pharmacy with a 24-hour service, the address of which is displayed on the doors of other pharmacies.

Personal Safety

Petty crime is the only likely problem travellers will face, although the big cities have their no-go areas at night. Follow normal precautions: don't leave anything in a car; be careful with purses and wallets; don't wear ostentatious jewellery and use hotel safe deposit boxes. Remember that some inland areas are very poor, so bag snatching is more of a temptation. Sexual harassment is not generally a problem and as the streets are so busy at night, women travellers should feel safe walking around the resorts.

Emergencies

Policia Nacional: 091
Policia Municipal: 092
Emergency Medical Service: 061
Police Assistance (Tourist Attention), tel: 93 301 9060
The tourist police station at Rambla 43 is open 24 hours in the summer.

Etiquette

Topless sunbathing is acceptable on the beaches but more modesty is appropriate inland around lakes and in the national parks.
Visitors are advised to adopt the Spanish siesta routine; visiting sights and expecting to

have meetings during the early afternoon is not appropriate. Expect to have dinner late; most Spaniards only eat at 22:00 or 23:00 in the summer, earlier in the winter.

Language

Catalan is today the main language spoken by 10 million people worldwide. Many of its derivations are French and the written word looks like a mixture of French and Spanish. The spoken word, however, is harsher sounding than French or Spanish and some accents outside the city are very strong. Most signs and maps are now in Catalan, although some are in **Castilian** as well. Castilian speakers will still be understood as virtually all Catalans are bilingual. Business can be conducted in either language. **English** is also understood in business circles and by people working in service industries, although sign language may be necessary in some smaller shops, markets and in taxis.

GOOD READING

• Morris, Jan (1982) *Spain* (Penguin, London)
• Lorca, Federico García *Five Plays: Comedies and Tragicomedies and Selected Poems* (Penguin, London)
• Nonell, Joan Bassegoda *A Guide to Gaudí* (Edicions de Nou Art Thor, Madrid).
• Hughes, Robert (1992) *Barcelona* (Harvill, London)
• Hooper, John *Spaniards: A Portrait of the New Spain.*
• Richardson, John *A Life of Picasso* (Random House, London)

INDEX